A House in the South

A House in the South

Old-Fashioned Graciousness for New-Fashioned Times

FRANCES SCHULTZ and PAULA S. WALLACE

CLARKSON POTTER/PUBLISHERS

NEW YORK

Acknowledgments

To the friends and strangers who became friends who so graciously opened their homes to us, thank you. And for special assistance, great suggestions, and support, my thanks again to Molly and Henry Froelich, Elizabeth Locke, Elizabeth and Mark McDonald, Angele Parlange, and Caroline Wallace. And how about these photographs—WOW! Another round of applause for Chia Chong, Deborah Whitlaw Llewellyn, and Richard Leo Johnson and his incomparable sidekick Vernon McAllister. I must also restate the obvious: Janice Shay is a goddess, and Angela Rojas is a goddess-in-training. All the staff and good people at Design Press are a blessing, and Molly Rowe is just terrific. Maria Gagliano and the gang at Clarkson Potter are always a joy to work with. Thanks to Paula S. Wallace for her leadership, inspiration, talent, and energy, and for all she continues to give to the arts, the South, and the world. It is an honor to be your coauthor. And finally, I just have to thank the great small town of Tarboro, North Carolina, where I grew up. Tarboro taught and continues to teach me about what it means to be Southern, and how to hold that in my heart forever. —*Frances Schultz*

A talented and generous collection of individuals, couples, and families constructed this *House in the South*. Many, many thanks to all of you who enthusiastically and patiently shared your homes' inspiring designs, ingenious furnishings, and engaging stories. For so beautifully capturing the charm and grace of Southern living, my thanks goes to photographers Chia Chong, Richard Leo Johnson, and Deborah Whitlaw Llewellyn. Thanks, also, to Molly Rowe, Janice Shay, and Anna Burgard for their essential contributions to research, editorial, and artistic direction, and to Angela Rojas for her design work. Finally, my thanks to Frances Schultz, for her inimitable voice, which brings personalities within rooms and rooms within neighborhoods home. —*Paula S. Wallace*

Photograph Credits

Chia Chiung Chong: pages 9, 16–21, 28–29, 30 (right), 32–33, 48–64, 66, 74–82, 86, and 120–127

Costopulos: pages 83–85 and 87

Ben Dashwood: page 65

Mark Hill: page 8. Courtesy Turner South. © TRENI. A Time Warner Company. All Rights Reserved.

Richard Leo Johnson: pages 3, 6, 22–27, 30 (left), 31, 71, 96–119, and 142–157

Deborah Whitlaw Llewellyn: pages 10–15, 34–41, 42–47, 67–70, 72–73, 88–95, and 128–141

Library of Congress Cataloging-in-Publication Data is available on request.

ISBN-13: 978-0-307-23651-7
ISBN-10: 0-307-23651-X

Printed in China

10 9 8 7 6 5 4 3 2 1

First Edition

Packaged by Design Press, a division of the Savannah College of Art and Design
PO Box 3146
516 Abercorn Street
Savannah, GA 31402
www.designpressbooks.com

Design Press Production Team:
Editorial: Anna Burgard, Molly Hall, Gina Marshall, and Molly Rowe
Design: Dove McHargue, Andrea Messina, Angela Rojas, and Janice Shay
Stylists: David W. Bush, Brian Carter, Natalie Evans, and Rebecca Gardner
Photography: Chia Chiung Chong, Catherine Hunsburger, Richard Leo Johnson, and Deborah Whitlaw Llewellyn

For my mother, the incomparable Ruth Clark; my dashing father, Jackson Schultz; family friend Columbus ("Lum") Mayo; my sister's father-in-law, J. B. Fuqua; and my favorite cousin, Tom Grainger, all of whom have left their earthly Southern homes since I began work on this book two years ago. May the heavens shine brighter with all that you are (and that's a lot), and may our hearts and homes, Southern and otherwise, be always warm with your memory.

—Frances Schultz

For my husband, Glenn,
whose designs tell many stories
of humor and grace,
of style and ingenuity,
of living in the South.

—Paula S. Wallace

Contents

Introductions

It may not be what you think. Having written about houses for longer than I want to say, I find I still have plenty to learn—even about houses like the one I grew up in. Yes, the South is about moonlight and magnolias, and our gleaming white columns stand tall to this day. But most of us don't live at Tara and never will. What was gone with the wind, though, is only part of the story. Times have changed, to be sure, and yet aspects of Southern living remain timeless. We Southerners are a tenacious lot, and we take home pretty seriously.

Which is not to say we all have serious houses. Or serious books about them, for that matter. This one, for example, does not claim to be a definitive tome of Southern architecture or design; it merely offers a range we find interesting, beautiful, clever, or charming. Oh, and pretty. We still like pretty in the South.

But what was interesting to me in talking and then writing about these houses is that the interesting-beautiful-charming part often came last. What came first was what the house was, its history and heritage, or its colorful stories. Then what came next was what the house was hoped to be, and that was always "gracious and warm." The word "eccentric" also turned up with unsurprising frequency. Quite often, too, did "hospitality" and the perceived welcoming attributes of a house's design.

The porch, for example, is how a Southern house can hug you. Everybody talked about porches. Turned outward, reaching toward you, the porch says, "Come on in." It protects and embraces; it offers shade and rest. In spite of air-conditioning and bugs and everything else, Southerners still love the outdoors and want their houses to relate to it.

So we track a little sand or mud inside, and there's dog hair on the sofa. A chair might need covering or the silver a little polish. We'll think about that tomorrow. Meanwhile, what can I fix you to drink? As my friend Ryan Gainey says, "It ain't just the accent. It's the attitude."

We hear a lot today about how houses are expressions of ourselves. Southern style today is an evolving aesthetic, at liberty to plumb the past and reinterpret it on its own terms. Southerners' tendencies to look to their roots, both individually and collectively, might nowadays be less for validation than for inspiration. The appeal of "Southern-ness" is not in stereotype or status, but in gentility—and a connection to something soulful. That's what these pages bring home for me. I'm not sure that can be photographed, but I hope you get the picture.

—Frances Schultz

When I reflect on the quintessential Southern dwelling, childhood memories of the Atlanta home of Jessie Corinne Ward Fleming flood my mind. Called Rinnie by her friends, she adopted me as her unofficial grandchild because from the time I was born until I was two, my parents lived in her backyard guesthouse. Even after our family bought a cottage a few streets away, we remained very close to Rinnie—my father helped prune her dogwoods, my mother would set her hair on Saturdays, and I would ride the bus with Rinnie downtown on shopping excursions . . . both of us wearing our gloves and carrying our purses.

Rinnie's tall white Victorian house began with a large front porch, complete with a wide, painted swing and a row of rockers. All the rooms had high ceilings and generous proportions. The main living rooms gently flowed into each other, and the bedrooms and kitchen were announced by tall doors with transoms.

The most important room in the house was the dining room, of course—partly for ceremonial reasons, partly because it was at the center of everything. One side of this spacious room functioned as a library, with expansive windows and a fireplace. Comfortable, low, upholstered armchairs for relaxing were guarded by crooked floor lamps for easy reading. On the other side of the room, a big, round dining table was illuminated by a large chandelier suspended by gold silk cords. Closets near the table concealed china serving pieces and crystal. She had lovely linens, indeed, yet more impressive than everything else were her place settings—we all had our own saltcellars, complete with tiny spoons. I don't remember Rinnie making ordinary, everyday food, but she did prepare special dishes like tomato aspic, ambrosia, fig preserves, Japanese fruitcake, bourbon balls, and—my favorite—Russian tea. She specialized in small celebrations.

Because she sewed, Rinnie had pretty curtains, bed skirts, and pillows, which adorned her home and contributed to the comfortable, gracious environment. I always admired her quilting and the fancy French knots with which she embellished the monograms on her handkerchiefs.

I remember Rinnie's home being cool and peaceful. A native of North Carolina, she seemed to bring a certain mountain airiness to her city residence, as well as her own kindness, generosity, and gentle spirit—intangibles that permeated her home just as surely as any architectural features. So many aspects of Rinnie's home are veritable badges of honor in Southern abodes: porches, gardens, the importance of food and dining, as well as life's niceties, such as hand embroidery and silver handed down from mother to daughter. As you join in a ramble through some of my favorite Southern homes, you may see glimpses of Rinnie every now and again, or someone equally special to your own memories of houses in the South.

—Paula S. Wallace

When you walk

through that gate you

leave the other

world behind . . .

ABOVE: In spring, Ryan Gainey's front porch is nearly overgrown by a cascade of pink climbing Cecile Brunner Cherokee roses.

OPPOSITE: The plates and chargers are Gainey's own designs. A portrait of Gainey by Robert Rausch hangs above a primitive antique cabinet. The mosaic hurricane lanterns are from Pier 1 Imports; the pierced tin lanterns, from Mexico.

The Gainey House

Decatur, Georgia

I just can't write about Ryan Gainey's house like I write about anybody else's. For one thing, it just isn't like anybody else's; then of course, neither is he like anyone else. My description of him in *Atlanta at Home* some years ago still holds true: garden designer, artist, epicure, philosopher, sybarite, visionary, prima donna, pain in the neck, genius, worldly sophisticate, small-town Southern boy. I would add to that now, true as it was then, friend. And if home is a reflection of self, Gainey's acre in Decatur, Georgia, is all that and more.

But one must begin with the garden, because it is where Gainey himself begins. It is a series of gardens—actually, garden "rooms"—formed by lavish borders, a parterre, a potager, an oval garden, rose arbors, and, most recently, *Il Jardino Echo*, a stunning miniature Italian Renaissance garden that Gainey created for the Southeastern Flower Show. Once there was even a small, swept, dirt yard, in homage to the rural South Carolina sandhills Gainey grew up in. That bit, alas, has been repurposed as a parking spot for Gainey's custom-made reproduction "woody" station wagon, but that's another story.

With its profusion of plants, trees, flowers, arbors, vines, and shrubs, one could quite understandably overlook the actual abode. Gainey tells the story of a young lady who used to bring her elderly father to visit there. One day the man greeted Gainey and asked, in all seriousness and surprise, "Oh, when did you get a house?"

It had been there all along, of course, but Gainey acquired the simple bungalow-style house, along with

several greenhouses and a barn, around 1982, buying it from a family who had operated a wholesale flower business there since the early 1900s. As Gainey continued his home's horticultural legacy and began transforming the property into one of the South's most spectacular gardens, his star continued to rise as one of the South's premier floral and landscape designers.

To say that his is the quintessential Southern house—and I would say it—might depend on your definition of "quintessential Southern house." But if this book conveys nothing else, I hope it is that the Southern home is less about architecture and design than it is about attitudes and ideas.

Of course some Southern houses—like some Southerners themselves—can be fancy; but the good ones are not "highfalutin." They are down to earth, we like to say, and we mean it as a compliment. Gainey's house, like Gainey himself, is down to earth but also of the earth—and at the same time of another world. (Southerners are perversely proud of their paradoxes.)

"When you walk through the gate you leave the other world behind, and it's a wonderful thing," he says. "I've created my own paradise and I live in it, in harmony with myself, with nature, and with my family. My whole house is filled with family," he says, not exaggerating. Old family photos and mementos cover many a surface in Gainey's home, some artfully assembled in collages. There is even a box that lights up when its little screen door is opened to reveal a photograph of his grandmother, reminding Gainey of when she used to watch him and his brother play "and make sure the rooster in the chinaberry tree didn't jump on our heads." His collection of turquoise jewelry and Native American basketry harkens to ancestry as well; Gainey's great-great-grandmother was part Cherokee.

"If it doesn't have a story, it's not worth repeating," he says, meaning everything in his house has a story behind it. Some are no doubt told and retold on his porch, an essential Southern exterior room created partly for that purpose. Another place for storytelling is around the supper table, and Gainey has further obliged hospitality by giving over his living room to a second dining area.

Most of his furnishings are artfully handwrought, honest, elemental: iron chandeliers and rustic wooden chairs; terra-cotta urns and cotton tablecloths. Like the magnolia leaves lining Gainey's sitting room ceiling, some edges fray, the paint peels in places, and yet you would not call it shabby. Quite the contrary; it is deceptively soignée. A loving paean to the past defiantly relevant in the present, this is a house endearingly homey, deeply personal, outright eccentric. The man doesn't even own a microwave, for heaven's sake. (But he does have a cell phone. Anachronism, after all, need not exclude convenience.)

As Southerners, Gainey says, "We are a great people, and we are different from anybody else in the world. People in Europe love us and it ain't just the accent. It's the attitude." —*F.S.*

ABOVE: A warm, tiny kitchen is unmarred by modern conveniences, but the Canadian brand Heartland stove is a vintage design and was installed in 2000, replacing the existing 1926 model.

LEFT: Like other rooms of the house, the guest room has a painted geometric design on the floor. A distressed, painted table displays Gainey's collection of Native American basketry. The portrait of Gainey is by Amelia James.

OPPOSITE: A primitive Haitian crucifix adorned with Gainey's Navajo turquoise jewelry watches over the study. The ceiling is covered in magnolia leaves from Gainey's garden.

ABOVE: A perennially award-winning
exhibitor in the Southeastern Flower
Show, Gainey created a scaled, miniature
Italian Renaissance garden for one
year's entry.

OPPOSITE: The back porch is fully
furnished with sturdy twig rockers,
tables, and lamps—for reading stories
or just tellin' 'em. (And that screen door
slams just like it's supposed to.) The
Potted Plant was the name of Gainey's
erstwhile retail establishment in Atlanta.

The spirit,

mood, and color

of a space should

begin with art.

The Wallace Residence
Amelia Island, Florida

A beach condo can be so attractive to an active family— the ability to throw on a bathing suit and a big hat before opening the door right onto the beach, the convenience of swooping in and out without any hassle, the feeling of security and the luxury of a well-kept pool. Yet the sterility of a towering complex is often standoffish. In the realm of beach living, the condo is (more often than not) anonymous. So, when my husband, Glenn, and I purchased one on Amelia Island a few years ago, we had quite the designer's challenge ahead: how to turn a condo into an unclichéd beach getaway that exudes Southern hospitality, casual liveliness, and contemporary charm.

In my mind, a hospitable home is a comfortable home. The colors, furniture, and environment should be just as cordial as the people who live inside. So, to create fresh, amiable compositions, we took traditional ideas and reinvigorated them with new sophistication.

In the master bathroom, a worn and unattractive breakfront experienced its renaissance thanks to a can of bright blue paint. And, as a result, this once dull, retired piece of furniture now has personality and provides perfect storage for towels and soaps.

But interior rejuvenation isn't just about painted revival. It's about imagination, about thinking outside of the tried-and-true paradigms of interior design. It's about taking something meant for one purpose and supplying it with new meaning. Take quilts, for instance. Families all over the world (specifically, here in the American South) have old quilts, tattered from

ABOVE: With a lovely view of Amelia Island's quiet beach, this weekend and summer retreat is perfect for a busy family.

OPPOSITE: A corner composition adds drama and youthful energy to a little girl's room. Floating paper vellum dresses by artist Amanda Leibee dance above a bed dressed in old quilts and vintage linens.

decades of love, passed down from generation to generation. Those quilts connote heritage and warmth—heaven forbid, our mothers told us, we should ever throw them away. In our condo, while we kept older quilts at the feet of our beds—one, in particular, that my sister and I carried on picnics as children—on a whim, we also transformed new quilts into curtains.

While most Southern homes are built around inherited or lovingly collected treasures, because this condo was our second home, we outfitted it with lesser collectibles amassed over a short period of time. And because some pieces lacked rich pedigrees, we created compositions evoking stories *we* wanted to tell. In the living room, a conch shell crowns a book about mermaids. Atop a book about love, I placed a glass heart. Indeed, design is narrative as well. In a guest bedroom, a small dressing table is decoupaged with thousands and thousands of stamps pulled off Savannah College of Art and Design applications arriving from all over the

world. In the breakfast nook, a secondhand table is decoupaged with 1940s recipes. Around the table, curtains are tied back with children's life preservers—the perfect functional accessory for beach living. With a little ingenuity, simple compositions can become elaborate tales that spark the imagination and invite dynamic conversation.

Guiding us throughout the design process was our need to avoid that wonted "condo" air. We approached color as an opportunity to brighten a forlorn condo shell and to complement the powerful landscape with apple greens, periwinkle blues, clear reds. The contrast of bold black-and-white-check curtains with the black blinds is almost daring, fostering an inviting, intriguing environment for everyone who spends a weekend or summer. In the living room, red toiles and kilim rugs recall very traditional patterns, yet they are invigorated with a certain youth when placed against blue walls trimmed in bright white. While alone these patterns awaken a familiar nostalgia, together they lend a certain contemporary crispness that each element could never achieve on its own. Again, traditional ideas, reinvigorated.

LEFT: Threes are always more appealing than twos! The black-and-white stripes of the lamps form a visual echo of the black-and-white horizontal lines of the blinds. An old, unfinished quilt is used as a table topper.

OPPOSITE: The dining-living space is animated with vivid color and intriguing accents, such as this brass palm tree from the estate of Ben Morris, a long-time professor at the Savannah College of Art and Design, and vintage character dolls resting in a glass bowl. The paintings are by Beatrice Caracciolo.

Above all else, a hospitable home is infused with a sense of place created by pieces you love—books, mementos, gifts with personal relevance. For me, an evolved environment demands striking art. I firmly believe that the spirit, mood, and color of a space should begin with art. At the Savannah College of Art and Design, I'm constantly surrounded by the compelling work of students, alumni, faculty, and guest artists. So, interiors that Glenn and I design often feature the work of artists we know. Whether by an emerging painter or a famed photographer, art should be given pride of place and preeminent priority. —*P.S.W.*

ABOVE: Children's life preservers are the perfect tiebacks for window curtains at the beach. A flea market table is decoupaged with copies of old recipes. The mixed media is by Katie Runnels.

RIGHT: In the guest bedroom, a touch of fringe and expandable hat racks transform this quilt into a charming window treatment. Chinese baby shoes add an unexpected and very personal accent.

OPPOSITE: Vivid color and bright, white trim invigorate this dressed-down living room. Low, secondhand chairs are revived with white paint and red toile. Large gold letters found at a flea market become curious art when tastefully hung. The art below the letters is by Justine Holmes, Sarah Bain Gallery.

As modern as home might be . . . one never really abandons its old-fashioned sentiments . . .

ABOVE: In the foyer, a classic Warren Platner table from Knoll is the base for a trio of sterling mesh and crystal vases by Pampaloni. The painting in the background is by the nineteenth-century Belgian artist G. Linden, from the owners' collection.

OPPOSITE: In a curving, oceanfront, Michael Graves–designed building in Miami Beach, Atlanta designer John Oetgen defined spaces with a series of columns and created specially lit "cloud-like" ceiling cutouts to enhance the illusion of height. The custom dining table is by Oetgen Design; the sculpture is by Jedd Novatt, through Salander-O'Reilly Galleries in New York.

The Blount-Reynolds Residence
Miami, Florida

You can take the boy outta Alabama, but you can't take Alabama outta the boy. Montgomery native Joe Blount may live part of the year in a Michael Graves–designed, city-slick, modern apartment building in south Florida, but he keeps culinary reminders of where he's from on hand at all times. Longtime Blount housekeeper and cherished family friend Annie Ruth Means's sweet potato casserole, along with her homemade biscuits and bags of fresh-picked lady peas, are staples in Joe Blount and partner Craig Reynolds's freezer, and they wouldn't have it any other way. "When I run out of biscuits," Blount says, "Annie Ruth sends me more overnight." This is at least one instance where a modern convenience preserves an old-fashioned custom: the baking and eating of Annie Ruth's biscuits.

For as modern as a home might be, wherever it is, one never really abandons its old-fashioned sentiments, and Blount's sentiments about his native South run deep. Even in this high-rise, hyper-contemporary space, Blount picks out an element that reminds him of home, of the outdoors of his boyhood in rural Alabama. In the master bedroom is a wood-grained wallpaper that Atlanta designer John Oetgen had cut into blocks and applied so that the grain runs in opposing directions. "That wallpaper really speaks to me," Blount says, "of the trees and the earth where I'm from." And he realizes that connection to nature is one of the things here he loves most.

"I'm on the eighth floor, so it's not a jetliner view," he continues. "I have more of a sense of the earth, sea,

and sky together, and the Lord paints a portrait for me every day that changes with every moment. The play of light, the waves, the clouds, the palm trees, the birds flying around—it's mesmerizing for me. It's hard to leave."

True, for all its glass and gleaming terrazzo, there is a welcoming embrace. The place is cool but not cold; utterly sophisticated and yet inviting. Leather and upholstered furniture is comfortable and accommodating, and "basically Jean-Michel Frank–inspired," says Oetgen, invoking the classic French modernist as muse for many of his own furniture designs. Seating arrangements suit crowds

ABOVE: A leather screen adds dimension and masculinity to the low-key, monochromatic master bedroom. Cut and applied in squares, Nobilis wood-grained wallpaper reminds Blount of the Alabama woods he played in as a boy.

OPPOSITE: An Oetgen-designed corner banquette and gilded deco chairs from Maison Gerard in New York create a sleek, glam seating area. The pedestal and urn are from Treillage, New York.

ABOVE LEFT: A stunning work by South American artist Claudio Bravo commands one wall of the living room. The cane-backed teak chair is from the owners' collection.

ABOVE RIGHT: An eglomise mirror atop an Andre Arbus commode reflects the owners' collection of Pampaloni silver and crystal carafes.

RIGHT: The play of sea, sky, and sunlight creates an ever-changing vista outside as well as in, prompting designer Oetgen to choose neutral whites and grays for the interiors so nature does the coloring.

large and small, because Southerners being Southerners, there's always company coming.

Joining two apartments together, Oetgen opened up the rooms and defined respective areas with a series of columns. He gave the eight-foot ceilings more of a feeling of height by inscribing them with random circular cutouts—"like clouds," he says—with halogen lighting. "The whole vision was to bring the feeling of the ocean inside," he begins, "not with a maritime theme or a yachting motif, but with something more ephemeral." The blue glazing on the windows casts a watery hue over an interior palette predominantly of whites and grays, shimmering aquatic washes that advance and recede like the tides. The reflection in the polished floor creates an overall effect "like you are in an aquarium," Oetgen says. "John's choice of colors was brilliant," Blount adds.

But where aquariums are sealed containers, the Blount-Reynolds home is often open, with the four guest rooms almost constantly occupied. Blount and Reynolds bring Southern hospitality to wherever home happens to be. Somebody's got to eat all those biscuits. —*F.S.*

ABOVE: Slithering along the polished terrazzo floor is "Happy Snake" by Tom Otterness, through the Marlborough Gallery, New York. In the foreground, a Mies van der Rohe chaise in white leather. In the background, a classic Saarinen Tulip table surrounded by Mies van der Rohe chrome and leather chairs, all from Knoll.

RIGHT: A guest bedroom gets a nautical punch with a bright blue-and-white Nobilis stripe. Extending the upholstered headboard continues the pattern into the room to blend with the chair and curtains. The crystal lamp and antique bronze side table are from the owners' collection.

A capricious cottage with contemporary flair and that distinct Tybee panache.

ABOVE: Greg and Kelley Parker have transformed an historic Tybee cottage into a spacious beach home while keeping the "bones" intact ... and on display.

OPPOSITE: An iron lemon vine frames the doorway to the kitchen. The wood floors were painted by Shawn Semmler. The stools tucked beneath the zinc-topped table are from Chiang Mai, Thailand.

The Parker House

Tybee Island, Georgia

"Everyone told us to burn it down and start over," Greg Parker recalls. Extensive termite damage, uneven floors, and a bizarre floor plan that forced people to go out onto the porch in order to enter the bedrooms upstairs were just a few of the design challenges ahead. But the Parkers' steadfast commitment to historic preservation, and their dream of spending weekends and summers on Tybee Island's Back River, rang much louder than the skepticism of close friends. "We loved the bones, loved the history, and absolutely adored the setting," Kelley Parker says. And so began the renovation—or, reinvention—of a turn-of-the-century Tybee river cottage.

Tybee (meaning "salt" to the Native Americans who once inhabited the island) is the two-and-a-half-mile-long and two-thirds-of-a-mile-wide barrier island located just twenty miles east of Savannah. A cozy beach neighborhood, yes, but big things come in small packages. In the past two hundred years, Spain, France, England, the Confederate States of America, and the United States of America have all flown their flags over this coveted strip of beach. Unlike many beach towns, this one is still populated with those charming, vintage clapboard cottages, where screened wraparound porches are often more spacious than the interior rooms. And unlike most Southern beaches, oat-covered salt dunes still protect the homes from the winds and the waves.

But despite the historic Tybee allure, Greg and Kelley didn't think they could preserve everything and please everyone at the same time. "Although we loved its history and unparalleled location," Greg says, "the

LEFT: A zinc-topped sideboard from Menerbe, France, used as an upstairs bar leads into one of the home's additions: a casual living room surrounded by vibrant art and walls of glass that give the impression of actually sitting in the oak tree just outside.

BELOW: A statue of Buddha from Chiang Mai is regally perched against the glass wall.

OPPOSITE: Exposed beams and a painted floor add barefoot charm and understated character to a casual dining room atmosphere.

house as it was just didn't fit our lifestyle—three kids, their friends, our friends, dogs, and more." But Greg was persistent and confident (especially, he tells me, "after a few margaritas"). With the help of a local architect, he found a way to preserve the historic structure and create a weekend retreat that everyone could enjoy. It's an "outside-in" effect: rather than add on here, or tear down there, Greg and Kelley built around the home, keeping the original interior and exterior walls, windows, and roof over the upstairs porches intact.

The result? A capricious Tybee cottage with contemporary flair, personality plus, and that distinct Tybee panache. In an upstairs addition, for example, original clapboard exterior walls form one side of a hallway, while large panes of glass form the other. A weathered, shingled roof slopes down into a modish sitting room enclosed by glass walls. It seems as if the entire room is suspended in the air, held up only by the curling branches of a live oak tree just outside. To one side, a rustic painted horse found in Provence trots in place; to the other, a shimmering Buddha stands erect. Original paned windows in Greg and Kelley's room provide peeks of the porch, the dunes, and beyond. "It's a more intimate space than our formal home in town," Kelley says. "The kitchen ceiling is the floor of the kids' bedroom. It's uninsulated, so we can just rap a

ABOVE LEFT: Every summer, the Parker children roll their lemonade stand (a reproduction ice-cream chest) out onto the streets of Tybee Island.

ABOVE RIGHT: This casual side porch is a favorite lunching spot.

RIGHT: Exposed roof tiles in the hallway are vestiges of the home's original exterior, which now forms interior walls and clever architectural accents. The painted horse in front of a mixed media by Marcus Kenney was found in Provence.

OPPOSITE: A screened porch just off Greg and Kelley's bedroom looks out onto the front "yard" and the uninhabited Little Tybee Island. Natural sand dunes encircle a terrace down below, complete with a towering fireplace made from stacked Tennessee stone.

broomstick to get their attention. No need for inter-coms—simple, casual living is our Tybee mantra!"

Like most homes on the water, the back of the house is actually street-side, while the front of the home faces the water and the sand. Greg speaks of the "two different seasons" of the cottage. While the backyard reminds him of "a grandmother's home"—spreading branches of a huge live oak, dappled light on the grass, the scent of Confederate jasmine, old-fashioned moonflowers, and oyster shells embedded in the tabby footpaths—the front yard is "hip and beach-y," complete with an outdoor

fireplace, kayaks, and beach paraphernalia tucked between the dunes, sea oats, and tall bamboo. "It's a funky house," says Greg, "but it's the quirks that give it its charm." —*P.S.W.*

*I thought you
were crazy when
you painted that
house black . . .*

The Jones House

Atlanta, Georgia

"I thought you were crazy when you painted that house black, and now it's the prettiest house on the street," exclaimed a neighbor of Atlanta designer Benjie Jones. It isn't black, exactly, more a deep charcoal gray. Jones says he always liked the color; it reminded him of the weathered shingled houses in the Hamptons, of all the rarified Yankee enclaves. "I did it on a whim," he says, "and I knew it would look good with a terra-cotta roof." Okay . . . Southampton, meet North Georgia, where the designer is originally from.

The word "idiosyncratic" seems to come up a lot with Jones, or more to the point, with Jones's house in the tidy Atkins Park neighborhood. Comprising several blocks within Atlanta's Virginia-Highlands area, Atkins Park was designed by the famed Frederick Law Olmsted, who of course designed New York City's Central Park, as well as Atlanta's Piedmont Park. A lot of Yankees probably don't know that. But back to the idiosyncratic thing. When asked if he thinks the South might be populated with a disproportionate number of interesting souls, Jones answers no, though not convincingly so. "I do remember there was that episode of *Designing Women*," he begins, in which Julia Sugarbaker famously allowed as to how "in the South we're proud of our crazy people. We don't hide them up in the attic. We bring 'em right down to the living room and show 'em off!"

This is not to say that either Jones or his living room are crazy. But it is true, he says, "As I get older I just don't feel as much the need to conform." Jones's interiors are in

ABOVE: Atlanta designer Benjie Jones's Mediterranean-style house is painted a deep charcoal gray (as opposed to black), creating a dramatic contrast with the terra-cotta tile roof. Arches frame the nicely proportioned front porch, which Jones says was the reason he bought the house.

OPPOSITE: An exuberant mix of the unexpected, Jones's dining room comprises an octagonal, marble-topped table, painted Venetian chairs, and an iron-and-wood swan-necked garden bench. Jones separated the panels of an antique screen and mounted them to the walls. Their decorative painted borders were done by friend and art dealer Timothy Tew.

ABOVE LEFT: If walls could talk, couldn't chairs have ears? The late Greg Jordan apparently thought so when he came up with this tufted, upholstered design that Jones couldn't resist.

ABOVE RIGHT: The front porch is one of the reasons Jones says he bought the house, and his comfy wicker furnishings make it inviting nearly all year round. The painting hung on the woodpile is a classic, quirky Jones touch.

LEFT: In Jones's bedroom, a parcel gilt soleil makes a mighty fancy hat rack. The white-and-gilt bench is Italian Empire upholstered in black leather. In the foreground is a Melchior sculpture.

OPPOSITE: Jones thought his guests might enjoy the "shade" of a painted palm as they reclined in an unusual metal bed, probably from the 1920s.

fact highly sophisticated, but also deeply personal. "I do think Southern houses are more personal, so you can let them be a little more eccentric. I also think you can have mementos that fit in with your décor. Everything here doesn't have a pedigree," he continues, but everything he has, he really, really likes. It might be a hand-carved eighteenth-century Italian candlestick or a cockleshell from St. Simon's Island, or a fine Oriental carpet atop a humble sisal. A gilded French soleil hung with straw hats and baseball caps, or gingham-check curtains in lieu of conventional cabinet doors. "People look at these things and think they are novel ideas, but they are not. I remember a friend of mine's grandmother had curtains over her kitchen shelves instead of cabinets, which turns out to be decorative and happy to me."

Other touches in the house, however, bear Jones's own unmistakable signature. The strong and beautiful art collection hung with chain from a picture rail. The nailhead trim around butcherblock countertops. The master bed of painted fencing pipe. The insouciant mix of old and new. And yet nothing about the house shows off.

There's a thing against showing off in the South. Maybe because for so long, so many had so little. Ostentation was considered not only distasteful but unkind. Jones was generous to open his house for the very first Virginia-Highlands Christmas house tour a couple of years back, and was frankly surprised at the range of people who came through what he calls this "crunchy intellectual" kind of neighborhood, what with its proximity to Emory University. As he stood by in the background, watching and listening to the legions of paying visitors, he was more than gratified by his design for the house; he was heartened. "I met all kinds of people," he said, "and some of them 'got it' better than my friends, including some who looked at my Chinese export collection and called 'em dishes." An important collection, he says, may give a house credibility, "but I'm glad that's not the only thing my house has. It's got some kind of feeling they like—one that's not intimidating." One lady, he says, even asked him for his phone number, which he gave her. "And she calls me every now and then; 'I was just thinking about your house,' she says." And they'll visit awhile on the phone, in the continuing dialogue that is a Southern home. —*F.S.*

ABOVE: The kitchen's nailhead-trimmed counters and snappy aqua-black color scheme are citified, but its cheery gingham curtaining calls it back home.

LEFT: The ice blue–and-ebony background in the entry, living, and dining areas sets up a strong color theme throughout the house. Atop the Spanish armoire is a Kimo Minton sculpture from Timothy Tew. The carpet is Jack Lenor Larsen sisal.

LEFT: In a masterful master bath, Jones had the cast-iron tub declawed and designed for it instead a cradle of heart pine. An antique iron-rope bench holds bathtime reading material. The barnlike door repeats the shutter design, and painted shelving and baskets provide simple and ample storage.

OPPOSITE: In the living room, a classic Charles Eames Butterfly chair in black and white leather joins a traditional sofa. The skirted table displays the personal and the precious, including Jones's bronzed baby shoe, a photo of his mother, a Picasso ceramic plate, and an Isabelle Melchior bust.

Space,

unobstructed,

is such a

precious gem.

The Tenenbaum Loft

Savannah, Georgia

ABOVE: Native American pottery and a delicate maple chair complement the rustic slate floors.

OPPOSITE: A light and sophisticated living room, complete with Dunbar wingbacks, Barcelona chairs, and a chaise by Mies van der Rohe.

All the world over, the city of Savannah is renowned for her distinct Southern flair—for her beautiful historic district built around twenty-four tree-filled squares, her azaleas in the springtime, her mossy air of mystery and romance. With a lovely Southern drawl and sweet sweet tea, this hostess of the South is a modern-day historic preservation success story. That being said, it might seem oxymoronic to claim that one of her prized interiors is a sleek, spacious, and intellectually challenging loft. Perhaps ridiculous to declare that this loft pierces the heart of Savannah charm. Once in a while, however, a *rara avis* comes along.

"I'm not really Southern," Lorlee Tenenbaum announces. "I'm from Bismarck, North Dakota. Arnold's our Southerner." Arnold, her husband, was born and raised in Savannah, and after he met Lorlee in New York, the two married and moved to Savannah to raise their family. "Would you believe that we lived in an historic house, circa 1849, on Jones Street for more than thirty years?" Looking around this modish loft towering above the cobblestone streets and Civil War cemeteries . . . well, no. Jones Street is *la crème de la crème* of historic streets in Savannah. Tourists flock from all over the world to admire the antebellum architecture and to peek through wrought-iron gates into enchanting side gardens. "From the outside, our house on Jones was just like every other house on the street—old and traditionally beautiful. But in our mind, it was just a shell." Once inside, a parade of the untraditional greeted you at the door: funky patterns,

brilliant color, and contemporary art. "At first," Lorlee tells me, "besides 'She's not from here,' no one really knew what to say!"

But, then, a few years ago, with their children spread out all over the country, Arnold and Lorlee decided they were ready for a change of space. "We wanted something open and airy—a big, simple space to display our art and relax! We're grandparents now, you know."

After a long ride up the elevator—a rare experience in historic Savannah—a small entranceway opens onto an expansive living-cum–dining room.

BELOW: A natural wood stain, demure lighting, and fluffy white towels offer a spa-terrific feel to the master bathroom. The only color comes from small plants and a framed poster from the Wes Anderson film *The Royal Tenenbaums* (named after, not inspired by, *this* Tenenbaum family).

Sunlight floods through massive demi-lune windows. The views of Savannah and the Savannah River are mesmerizing. Despite the sophisticated Dunlap designs to the right and an Andy Warhol to the left, the panorama is without a doubt the centerpiece of the home. Space, unobstructed, is such a precious gem.

A Southern home, Arnold reminds me, "has nothing to do with the outer shell or the interior plan. It's about welcoming people inside and providing a place where they can relax and enjoy their visit." Unlike many rigid and intimidating modern interiors, Arnold and Lorlee's loft is uplifting and personal—a reflection of their passion for travel, art, and Native American craft. "We've spent our summers in Santa Fe since the children were young. It was inevitable that I would fall in love with Native American art," Lorlee says. Whether

ABOVE: An unparalleled view of historic Savannah from a living room window. Banquettes line the perimeter of the room to accommodate large numbers of guests.

RIGHT: Bowls by famed Georgia sculptors Edward and Philip Moulthrop complement the curvilinear design of a mahogany table.

ABOVE: A striking Pistoletto painting is the centerpiece of this highly textured bedroom setting. The lamps flanking the sofa are a gift from a daughter's trip to Hong Kong.

LEFT: The clean lines of Dunbar chairs add modern flair to old Savannah silver. A Navajo rug becomes contemporary art when hung above a Chinese prayer table. The Chinese and Native American artifacts were collected during the Tenenbaums' travels.

figures lined like soldiers on a shelf or small bowls mixed in with books, the Native American crafts look at ease amid fine modern art and slick contemporary shapes.

One glance at the dining room vignette and you understand. In the background, a Navajo rug hangs above a Moulthrop bowl, East Asian figures, and Native American pottery lined up on a Chinese prayer table. Posed in the corner is a papier-mâché gaucho from Spain. And in the foreground, old Savannah silver is centered on a 1960s Dunbar table. Beyond the sophisticated blend of clean contemporary lines, elegant antique curves, and rustic nativist shapes, what's most intriguing is the story evoked. It's as if the Tenenbaums have taken pieces of their life in Santa Fe and pieces of their life in New York, and from those created their castle in Savannah's sky.

Arnold and Lorlee are well-known philanthropists and gracious patrons of the arts who love to entertain in their home. Inviting a hundred guests up to their sophisticated loft is not at all recherché. And because of the expansive windows and alpine ceilings, there always seems to be ample room. A low, cushioned banquette lines the circumference of the living and dining area, inviting guests to sit comfortably, cocktail in hand, with the hostess of the South bustling down below. —*P.S.W.*

RIGHT: Natural light beaming from the living room windows illuminates the stark, sleek stainless steel in the kitchen. The mesh Bertoia/Knoll barstool provides casual kitchen seating without creating a visual barrier in a small space.

Just because something is framed with elegance doesn't mean that it has to be formal itself.

ABOVE: Poised in the historic district of Savannah, Susan Mason's home—complete with mustard trim and a red tin roof—is authentically Victorian. The brilliant colors infuse the entire block with pizzazz.

OPPOSITE: Sculptural stacks of cookbooks circle the rim of this nineteenth-century English table in the living room fit for a chic Georgia queen. Large animal prints on Susan's mother's old chairs truly pop when framed by a gold-leaf ceiling and va-va-voom purple walls.

The Mason House

Savannah, Georgia

Imagine a storybook Victorian home: flirtatious architecture, circular towers, and whimsical details, including a red tin roof and gingerbread trim. Poised on a busy corner in Savannah's historic district, Susan Mason's 1893 Victorian home is all that . . . and so much more. Beyond its pepper red double doors, a dazzling interior is revealed, bursting with personality and contemporary chic. "I love a Victorian house," says Susan. "They're so quirky—you can do absolutely anything with them." Perhaps, but only Susan could do *this*.

In the foyer, large canvases of contemporary art climb the walls along the stairwell. To the left is a double parlor with a round bay looking onto the street, where Susan has tucked a round dining table. The day we visited, the table, dressed in lime and aqua silk, was already set for dinner guests she expected later that evening. The second parlor is more like an enchanting boudoir for this Savannah doyenne—deep purple walls, a gold-leaf ceiling, vintage yellow curtains, and a panoply of animal prints. It's seductive, outrageous, glamorous, and, well, quintessentially Susan. At the rear of the home sits the personal kitchen of one of Savannah's top chefs. I almost want to peek into the drawers and crack the cabinets to see what little secrets this *étoile* of entertaining might conceal in her very own *cuisine*. Ironically, or perhaps not, Susan's kitchen is rather petite, with ash gray painted cabinets and walls of deep blue swimming pool tile. A framed, personalized cartoon of a hobo is perched on the corner of the counter. It reads: "I made mine catering!"

As a celebrated Southern caterer, Susan participates in more weddings than a gaggle of sorority girls from Ole Miss. "A Southern mother starts planning her daughter's wedding the day the daughter's born. And daddies, well, they still pay for the grand soirees, of course." In fact, Susan astutely traces Southerners' reverence for heritage and our tendency to surround ourselves with decorative, functional objects back to the wedding tradition—or, more accurately, to the silver and crystal and china received as wedding gifts. "Brides still select three sets of china," Susan tells us as we take mental notes—one would be a fool not to follow Susan's advice on anything dealing with etiquette or place settings. "She has her everyday, her in-between, and her most exquisite. So, even young couples begin housekeeping with lovely things that they display and use daily."

As we climb up the stairs, the vigorous colors of the parlors and kitchen recede to restful tones of white, cream, taupe, and gray. It's spare and serene—the perfect haven for sleep and ideation. In her bedroom, narrow French doors open to a private balcony laced with heady jasmine. The linens are stark white, loosely draped across the bed. Well-fluffed monogrammed pillows are stacked high. It

ABOVE: Years of thank-you notes blanket Susan's "Me" board on her bedroom wall.

LEFT: A round dining room table tucked into the bay window is set with Waterford crystal and a riot of color. Behind the table hangs a portrait of Susan's daughter, Christine.

OPPOSITE: Soft colors and whimsical organdy curtains around this French bed frame in the master bedroom create a soothing retreat after a busy day's work.

was a breezy afternoon when we visited, and the sheer organdy curtains fluttered in the wind around her bed. A striking gown and stunning jewelry from a dinner party the night before lay tossed across a low trunk. "I have a frenetic lifestyle," Susan admits, "so when the day is over, I love nothing more than to crawl into my crisp white sheets and relax in solitude."

It's no secret that Southern women, men, and even small children have at least one set of personalized stationery. But, more likely, they have several. The handwritten note holds a certain prestige in Southern society, even in an age when "lesser" modes of communication—like the cell phone and e-mail—are used more frequently than a toothbrush. There's just something about putting pen to paper, literally, that conveys more compassion, friendship, and personality than any elaborate gift or phone conversation. That being said, personal stationery adorned with a variety of initials—Southerners do indeed have a way with monograms—decorates one of Susan's bedroom walls. "Susan, the word last night: 'This is the best meal ever served at the Telfair Ball,'" one reads. And, "I love my little angel of courage," reads another. Then, "As usual, perfect," with a big smiley face. "It's just sort of . . . what would you call it? . . . my 'Me' board! So every morning I can look at it and say, 'Oh, dear. I am fabulous.'" And, indeed, she is.

Susan converted the second bedroom upstairs into a spacious office with stacks of cookbooks and scattered relics of her annual pilgrimages to France. The smaller, third bedroom was transformed into a luxurious dressing room and closet, dripping with purses, belts, hats, and pearls—a feminine retreat

par excellence!

While the artwork, colors, and other collectibles in her home seem to be an extension of Susan's ebullient personality, what truly captures her verve are the hundreds of framed pictures dressing every single tabletop. Pictures of her two children, of a wonderful party in Palm Beach, a wedding here, a dinner with friends there, all framed in perfectly polished silver. And perhaps that's just it: just because something is framed with elegance doesn't mean that it has to be formal itself. Though externally some Southern homes may appear prim and proper and extremely *raffiné*, once inside, it's all about comfort and enjoying your time . . . together. —*P.S.W.*

LEFT: Vivid color, a mirror framed with old shutters, a vintage porch swing, and a wicker table animate this petite balcony just off Susan's office.

Monograms

We Southerners have honored our family names, commemorated memorable events, and refined our possessions with decorative monograms for centuries. And we're in very good company, for the desire to create personal logos dates back thousands of years. The Chinese stamp *chop*—the iconic carved stone seals dipped in bright red paste—to sign their paintings and documents. The Japanese use *kamon*—family crests designed with stylized animals, plants, and flowers—to mark their kimonos, samurai swords, and paper lanterns. Europeans have used heraldry, or family shields, on rings that were pressed into wax, family silver, and saddles taken into battle for centuries.

A true monogram is formed when two or three letters are joined to become a unified shape. Gracefully entwined curves, mirrored forms, and interesting spatial relationships between the letters are all hallmarks of a carefully rendered design. Whether crisp modern lines or curlicues are drawn, the synergy of the letterforms elevates them beyond mere identification marks—the best are works of art in themselves.

One of the most famous monograms is Queen Victoria's crowned V-R (Victoria Regina), which emblazoned medals, carriages, and a host of more mundane objects throughout her empire. It appeared on so many items, in fact, that the upper and middle classes' eagerness to stitch and etch initials onto surfaces of their own grew into what some have called a "monogramania." From that era on, monograms were seen not only inside grand estates, but in cottages and town homes with possessions fine enough to adorn. Once needlework became a part of a young girl's education (beginning with cross-stitching samplers), brides-to-be were expected to embroider sheets and tablecloths for their trousseaus with their own initials (it wasn't until relatively recently that the "blended" monograms of the husband's and wife's initials were stitched together in celebration of their union).

Today, oversized monograms are a growing trend—those for shower curtains, bedspreads, and pillows are running as large as twelve inches. And while tone-on-tone letters are the traditional favorite, there is also a movement toward bold color combinations. Practical and decorative, historic and modern, monograms are a reflection of taste, individuality, and the importance of family heritage. Whether on sterling mint julep tumblers, silk pillows, or cotton stationery, they add a touch of refinement and panache to any home. —*P.S.W.*

Defying what anyone might preconcieve as a "Southern" house.

The Ransom House

ABOVE: A pair of carriage house doors Kate Ransom saw in France inspired the design direction of her house in Tennessee. She never did say what inspired the Shoney's Big Boy . . . an appetite for eccentric Southern icons, perhaps.

OPPOSITE: Sunlight pours into the formal living room, whose taupe-and–ice blue color scheme complements the trees and sky surrounding it, as Ransom intended.

The arrival at Kate Ransom's Nonesuch is worth the somewhat precipitous approach up a steep, winding, tree-lined drive. So many trees in fact that the Nashville, Tennessee, house is a bit of a surprise. Truth to tell, the house is a bit of a surprise anyway, rather defying what anyone might preconceive as a "Southern" house. Or maybe winking at that preconception is a better way to put it. With its hipped roof, central block, and symmetrical wings, the silhouette is classic Georgian. But then French doors, wrought-iron balconies, delicate balustrades, and unusual oculus windows hint more at the Tuileries than Twelve Oaks—Beaux Arts with a pinch of Cape Dutch, and a certain Continental je ne sais quoi. Defining her vision through architect John Tackett, Ransom didn't set out to build some wonderful period house; she set out to build a wonderful house, period. A serious house that isn't. A house that is above all "comfortable and welcoming," she says. The word "whimsical" comes up a lot. "And you know what really inspired it?" she asks. "A pair of doors I saw on a carriage house in France."

Around to the side are those doors reproduced, heralded by (speaking of whimsy) the blue-eyed, pompadoured, potbellied eminence of Shoney's Big Boy himself, holding his eponymous burger triumphantly aloft. (For the uninitiated, Shoney's restaurants have been a fixture on the landscape of Southern highways for years.) "I had plans to have outfits made for him for holidays and special occasions," Ransom explains matter of factly, "but I never have gotten around to it."

Some whims are best left in their idea form. But the barn doors were a substantial whim, enough to build a house around.

An exaggeration of course, but the shape and scale of the doors appealed, as did their "French feel," a stylistic inclination not unknown in the American South. In larger cities, especially, the last twenty years or so have seen a tremendous surge in affection for French designs—commensurate perhaps with the general public's discovery of Provence and increased international travel in general. But if

Ransom's barn doors are a nod to the provincial, her interiors are *de la ville,* in a confident blending of fine French period pieces, English florals and poufy pillows, lovely prints and decorative pieces, and pure Southern comfort.

Family heirlooms and photographs, softly gleaming silver, and collections of botanical watercolors, Chinese ceremonial robes, perfect perfume bottles, and embroidered linens reflect the refined, sophisticated taste of one who grew up with beautiful things and then went on to

learn their provenances. Ransom studied interior design, has traveled extensively, and lived abroad, all the while searching, observing, and, occasionally, acquiring.

All these prized objects d'art demand a context worthy of them, however, and for that Ransom turns to Nashville designer David White. "I do the background," White says, "and Kate finishes." In the downstairs public rooms White's so-called backgrounds are intentionally composed of mainly neutral colors, so as not to compete with his client's beloved views of trees and sky outside. The bedrooms, nighttime spaces, are more colorful and feminine.

White and Ransom have collaborated for nearly thirty years. They practically finish each other's sentences—occasionally bickering like old married folks (which they aren't) and teasing like old friends (which they are). Take that stunning hot pink dining room, for example. Ransom adores it and would have nothing to do with an "informal eating area,"

ABOVE: Occupying an alcove between foyer, living room, powder room, and bar are a chartreuse jacquard-covered Louis XVI settee and a set of watercolors on rice paper depicting Asian ceremonial warrior garb—"Very theatrical," says Ransom.

RIGHT: Above the master bath's delicate marble mantel are silk embroidered miniatures of Chinese robes, acquired by Ransom in Shanghai. The vanity was her great aunt Reba Gray's.

OPPOSITE: A guest room balcony overlooks the front courtyard and guesthouse. The floor lamp belonged to the owner's grandmother and was originally lit by gas. The chintz curtains are from Claremont, London.

strongly suggested by all and sundry. "I live in every room of this house, and I use my dining room as it was intended," she says. But it is an interior room when its doors are closed, opening as they do to corridors on either side. Mirroring the doors seemed a good idea but also "a lot of information." Too much mirror, too much detail, too much with a fully set table surrounded by presumably decorative guests. So the challenge would be to create a surface that was reflective—beautiful in the candlelight but soft around the edges so as to slightly blur the images. Ransom's suggestion was to put antique mirror beneath panes of wavy glass— ingenious by all accounts. Except perhaps her designer's: "Looks like aluminum foil to me," he announced. And then, as we like to say in the South, they both "fell out" laughing. —*F.S.*

RIGHT: Fuchsia is a fabulous color for a dining room—stimulating to the senses and flattering to the complexion. An extraordinary carved and gilded nineteenth-century French mirror from Tom Hayes in Atlanta hangs above a marble-topped Italian commode from Orion Antiques, Dallas. The chandeliers are antique Venetian. On the arched sliding doors, wavy glass panes backed by antique mirror produce a soft, watery reflection.

Graciously

proportioned rooms

jive to a vibrant

bohemian chic.

ABOVE: The Gothic Revival architecture of the Eaton House is certainly appropriate to its former role as a rectory.

OPPOSITE: On a porch that wraps around three sides of the house, an old-timey metal glider and chair create a welcoming spot to sit and visit.

The Eaton House

Nashville, Tennessee

Southerners love nothing if not a good story, so it follows naturally enough that Southern houses have stories, too, particularly if they've been around awhile. This charming white clapboard house in Nashville, Tennessee, even looks like something from a storybook, and it lives up to its promise. Owner Karin Coble Eaton pulls an old shoe box down from a shelf and begins carefully to show and tell. There's a tattered epaulet from a Confederate's uniform; a Union soldier's "U.S." belt buckle; a brittle *Traveler's Guide to Niagra Falls;* old marbles; an ivory toothbrush—all a child's forgotten keepsakes, and poignant pieces of the past. The cache was discovered squirreled away in a wall when Karin and her husband, Robin, began to renovate several years ago, having acquired the house in 1994. "The Battle of Nashville was fought near here," she says, by way of explaining the Civil War souvenirs, and these must have been some little boy's scavenged treasures.

Listed on the National Historic Register, the Eatons' house dates to 1854, built by an Anglican minister. As it happens, the minister's wife was also the daughter of an Anglican bishop who was the founder of the Episcopal church in Tennessee. And though there were a few secular owners in between, the house served as a rectory again a century later. The owners prior to the Eatons were the Wards. Thomas Ward was minister of the venerable Christ Church Episcopal, downtown. Eaton says the small covered porch off what is now the music room and library once served as a practice pulpit. Or that was the story, anyway. Eaton confesses she thinks

LEFT: Sunlight streaks across the front porch and spills into the entry. The large Gothic doors are original to the 1854 structure, as is the miniature chair, which a previous owner wanted to remain with the house.

BELOW: The door to the library–music room was rumored to be a "practice pulpit." Through the door is Karin Eaton's great-grandfather's banjo. The chandelier is from her company, Ironware International.

OPPOSITE ABOVE: Prints from the famed Alfred Stieglitz 291 gallery surround an exclamatory graphic from Hatch Show Prints, located in the Country Music Hall of Fame and longtime printers of the Grand Ole Opry posters.

OPPOSITE BELOW: Karin's husband Robin's base fiddle rests in a corner of the foyer. A primitive painted cabinet holds an assemblage of treasures. The painting at bottom right above the cabinet is a self-portrait by Robin's grandmother Bernice Fernow. The rug was purchased during a trip to Istanbul.

it may have been "one of those myths." True Southerners are not wont to have their stories obscured by facts.

The (confirmed) ecclesiastical connection is certainly appropriate, however. The house's Gothic Revival style, so commonly seen in the South's many churches, was particularly popular at the time of construction and may have been in part an antidote to the strict constraints of classical architecture that had so firmly taken hold on Southern soil. With its pointed arches, steep gables, lacy bargeboards, and wide verandas, the Gothic Revival style gained momentum with a larger romantic movement reflected in the South's culture and society. The florid nineteenth-century writings of Sir Walter Scott epitomized the region's ingrained notions of aristocracy and upheld its chivalrous standards—noble ideals that were embraced by Southerners of the antebellum era and that frankly in some measure linger to this day, which is not all bad. Perhaps more than any other region in the country, the South was and is romanticized by its stories and houses as well—for which architecture is an eloquent raconteur.

Eaton has been lucky enough to hear some of her house's old tales. "A woman whose grandfather lived here told me about how she roller-skated on the porch," which was a bright spot in what then was an otherwise, to her young eyes anyway, rather dreary place. So when the woman visited Eaton—who was a bit nervous at the prospect—the woman exclaimed, "Oh my dear, I am so happy to see you have infused this house with life!" Indeed with life (teenaged daughter, Alex, and friends), music (father and husband, Robin, songwriter, composer, and producer), and style (Karin, former fashion

TOP: In the master bath, a trio of leaded and stained-glass windows casts acorn-and-oak-leaf and rose-and-thistle motifs across Eaton's collection of seashells and heart-shaped rocks from all over the world.

ABOVE: A once-working fire hydrant enjoys new status as sculpture by one of a pair of old church pews on the porch.

model and Karl Lagerfeld muse, now CEO and designer of Ironware International, the prosperous artisanal ironworks company she founded, which specializes in light fixtures and bed frames hand-forged in Normandy).

With so much talent and energy under one roof, it's no wonder the high-ceilinged, graciously proportioned rooms jive to a vibrant bohemian chic. Pillows and spreads in a mix of patterns and textures relax a serious Victorian sofa as effortlessly as they dress up a comfortably worn leather couch. Leopard-seated dining chairs tuck perfectly happily under a prim, crocheted tablecloth. A collection of books and artifacts ranges from a signed galley of *Cold Mountain* to *The Canterbury Tales;* from an antique stone Buddha to Karin's grandfather's banjo to Robin's bass fiddle. An art collection embraces the gamut from African sculpture to Alfred Stieglitz prints to Robin's grandmother's exquisite miniature portraits. A pool table has recently taken up residence in the living room. Oh, and there's a fire hydrant on the porch.

Of course there's a fire hydrant on the porch. It wouldn't be as good a story without it. "It was a Christmas gift from Robin and Alex two years ago. It was by the fireplace in the dining room, but I needed a break from it so I took it onto the porch," Eaton recounts. And who's to say where the fire hydrant or the story of this great old house will go next? It is a story still in the telling, still in the listening, still in the living. —*F.S.*

Decorative Iron

A lovely and distinguishing feature of Southern architecture is its decorative ironwork, found most notably, but by no means exclusively, in Savannah, Charleston, and New Orleans. There is visual poetry in the metal's meandering curves and spirals, and motifs evocative of the Southern landscape are often incorporated: magnolia leaves, palmetto fronds, corn husks, and even cotton plants. Wildlife, too, might be worked into the design: a dolphin becomes a waterspout; a griffin, a boot scraper.

As it became more available to Southern builders in the 1800s, iron quickly surpassed mere industrial use. Iron's strength, resistance to rust, and malleability made it a material that could be both decorative and functional. Houses in town might have iron fencing as much for ornament as for security, and an elaborate iron gate afforded some privacy without blocking the view of appreciative passersby.

People commonly confuse "wrought iron" with "cast iron," however. The former is actually wrought, or worked, by a blacksmith; while the latter is made by castings and more easily mass produced. By the early nineteenth century, most wrought iron had been superseded by cast iron, which was not quite as durable but considerably more versatile, and substantially less costly.

Balconies of iron appeared in Charleston as early as 1739. Wrought iron featuring scrolls, fleurs-de-lis, leaf and flower patterns, and spears flourished there through the eighteenth and nineteenth centuries. But as with that of many other early-American cities, much of Charleston's decorative iron was reforged into weaponry during the Revolutionary and Civil wars. The noted twentieth-century blacksmith Philip Simmons is credited with reinvigorating the three-hundred-year-old wrought-iron tradition in Charleston, and his protégés continue to adorn what he called "the Beautiful Lady." In Savannah, iron arrived in cotton ships as ballast. First used for monuments and fountains, it was soon shaped into railings for stairs, window guards, and the so-called "flying staircases" that spiral without the support of a wall. The best examples, however, are perhaps found in New Orleans. The French Quarter's Rue Royale, with its rows of black filigreed balconies welcoming breezes into Creole houses, is proud evidence of the New Orleans sobriquet "the City of Iron Lace."

Wrought or cast, ornamental ironwork is treasured in today's Southern cities and is a beautiful and enduring architectural homage to the past. —*F.S.*

Storied wear and tear adds more character than the finest bullion fringe.

ABOVE: This Gothic Revival home on Charleston Harbor has a rich history and perhaps a few friendly ghosts, but inside, it's full of young energy and contemporary soul.

OPPOSITE: An unexpected pairing of early American pieces and French art deco chairs designed by Paul Fallot add zing to this gracious drawing room. The caning of the Hepplewhite settee allows an unobstructed view into the library beyond.

The Faith House

Mount Pleasant, South Carolina

If you ask Elizabeth ("Muffie") Faith about the hurricane cross hanging above her bed—a not-so-uncommon feature in the coastal Carolinas—she'll tell you, "Hurricanes? We're used to those. What we need protection against are the ghosts! Honey, this house had a soul long before we arrived." Since 1850, this Southern Gothic charmer has housed a ferry captain, Civil War invalids, and families on summer retreat. There's no question, she's got soul(s).

When Muffie first laid eyes on Southwind, she looked right past the dilapidated structure and room after room of peeling paint. "She was a grand dame with regal bones that looked like she'd had the wind knocked out of her." Yet the house was poised on a bluff at the highest point in Charleston, and the twelve-foot windows and wide center hall offered sweeping views of Charleston Harbor. "Standing beneath the crumbling porch looking out to the marsh," Muffie says, "I thought, This is home."

But in order to *come* home, Muffie, an interior decorator who owns the shop ESD on Charleston's famed King Street, first had to *create* her home. Southwind was to become her pièce de résistance.

The original house had six common rooms arranged on two floors around a wide, central hall—no bathrooms, no closets, no kitchen. These "extra" spaces were all housed in small additions clustered around the main house. "I knew that renovation would be a personal process." But that's the great thing about the South—there's always a friend nearby that you grew up with who can trace your quirks and eccentricities back to grade

school. Someone who can help you accommodate family needs while honoring the historic lines of a Gothic Revival design. A personal project, indeed. So, Muffie called upon her favorite architect and childhood friend, Beau Clowney, to help her bring Southwind back to its original grandeur.

The new design nearly doubles the size of the house. And, rest assured, bathrooms and closets and a large kitchen are included. "I allowed the outdoor vistas to determine the room placement," Muffie explains. It seems that many Southerners, like Muffie, strive for a direct connection with their land—as if Southern pride is rooted in that exact place where you stand.

Throughout the home, Low Country references to land and lore abound. In the new living room, an entire wall of French doors opens to the marsh on one side and to a small side garden on the other, allowing the interiors to blend seamlessly with the exterior. The marsh-inspired colors on the walls and the texture of the sea grass rugs seem to be in constant conversation with the colors and textures on the other side of the window. Then, across the home in the hexagonal library addition, Muffie designed a ceiling that recalls that of the pavilion on Charleston's renowned Battery.

But while the gables and the transoms and manifestations of local lore may attest to the souls of days gone by, Muffie has without a doubt infused Southwind with soul that is all her own. "Styling a room according to one period just isn't my thing," she says of her personal predilection. "I believe you need to surround yourself with things you love—no matter if it's your favorite piece of art or a pair of old lamps tattered with years and years of love." Strolling into the drawing room, Muffie gazes at a pair of pheasant lamps, eyes glazed over with nostalgia. "I grew up with my grandmother sitting next to those bird lamps. And these shapely shades, although they're covered with unsightly rips and tears, I adore knowing that she made them. To me," she says pointing to the shades, "this is home." And most Southerners would agree: storied

wear and tear adds more character than the finest bullion fringe.

In a matter of steps, you can walk from a velvet walled "sit up straight" dining room to a large, casual kitchen adorned with country French antiques; from a seat in a prized art deco chair to a rocking chair on the back porch. "My home is about being comfortable in a space that could belong to no one else but my family. Whether we're entertaining for a black-tie affair or for a crew of fifth graders, I want my guests to be completely at ease."

To boil down Muffie's style, she's mastered the art of uncontrived elegance—architectural symmetry paired with off-kilter compositions, a mélange of styles that always seems to captivate and inspire. She's inventive, she's curious, and she's not afraid if this isn't perfectly aligned with that. "Life is tough," she declares, "we all need a bit of the unpredictable to keep it interesting." —*P.S.W.*

OPPOSITE ABOVE: A porch overlooking Charleston Harbor is enlivened by blending modern and traditional porch furniture. When Southwind was built in the 1850s, this was considered the front of the home.

OPPOSITE BELOW: From the living room, a screen door provides a perfect view of the water and the marsh. A long pier leads out to a dock where the Faiths house their boats.

RIGHT: Muffie's sentimental attachment to her grandmother's pheasant lamps illustrates the Southern reverence for family heritage and heirlooms.

Southern Kitchens

To tell you the truth, the modern-day Southern kitchen probably isn't that different physically from kitchens in other parts of America. But what comes out of 'em still probably is. Southern kitchens make me think of fried things—chicken, okra, green tomatoes, eggplant, oysters, bacon, peanuts. If you can eat it, you can fry it. Even if you can't eat it, you probably could if you fried it. Anyway, I think of those yummy fried whatevers sprinkled with salt and draining on greasy paper towels laid on top of brown bags, and how they had a way of disappearing before their appointed serving time. Smart cooks had to be quick hand-slappers and learned either to squirrel some away or just give in and make extra.

Even through hard times in the South, hostesses clung fiercely to the trappings and accoutrements of their (real or imagined) heritage, bravely keeping up the front of gracious hospitality until the real thing could return. Someone told me once of an old-time family cook who grumbled, "Dey was too much rattlin' of da silver for da few-ness of da food!"

The Southern kitchen gamely persevered, however, to produce some of the finest cooks, characters, and cookbooks in the land. Since Mary Randolph published the seminal *Virginia Housewife* in 1824, our kitchens have turned out the likes of Craig Claiborne, Paul Prudhomme, Emeril Lagasse, Edna Lewis, Martha Stamps, and others. Entire Junior Leagues of Southern cities have basked in the glories of their cookery books, and I swear if the building were burning I'd grab my *Charleston Receipts* right along with my velvet Elvis.

In the early Colonial days, in the South and elsewhere, the kitchens pretty much were the houses and everything else—living and sleeping rooms, too. As prosperity increased, so did the size of houses. To lessen the risk of fire and the inconvenience of cooking smells and commotions, kitchens in the eighteenth and nineteenth centuries were built apart from the main houses, as were smokehouses for curing meats, and milk houses for dairy storage.

But as modern convenience prevailed and practicality encroached, the kitchen moved back home. Once again the cooking hearth is the heart of family life, and houses today are often designed with that in mind. In many ways Southerners set themselves apart, but in this way we are like everybody else. Except we fry more. —*F.S.*

ABOVE: A chandelier crafted out of antique buttons hangs from a guest bedroom ceiling.

OPPOSITE: The modern glass column lamp is an effective foil for decadently ornate Italian daybed panels. The hurricane cross hanging above the bed is a common feature in Southern coastal homes forever at the mercy of Mother Nature.

PREVIOUS SPREAD: A kitchen perfect for casual dinners with friends or active fifth graders. Light pouring in from large corner windows illuminates the colorful glass organized on open shelves above the sink. Reclaimed beams, brick, and slate floors were designed to resemble the original kitchen that was detached from the main house.

A flair for gentlemanly pursuits remains alive and well.

Delta Plantation

Hardeeville, South Carolina

ABOVE: The enchanting approach to Delta Plantation, built in 1926, is a journey to the turn-of-the-century South.

OPPOSITE: In the mudroom, hand-colored lithographs by illustrator A. B. Frost hang on the pecky cypress walls. Functional shelving and wood pegs take the place of closets, elevating tall boots and hunting gear to the level of art.

Strolling down a dirt road that leads to Delta Plantation, it seems that time has evaporated into the canopy of Spanish moss overhead. "General William Sherman and his men marched right down this same road during the Civil War on their way into Savannah," John Cay reveals. "And just a few days later, he offered the city to President Lincoln as a Christmas present. Imagine that!" But the striking thing is, imagination's not required. If you attune your eyes to the distance, you see the dust still rising from the general's boots. It's uncanny how the past and present coexist side by side in many of today's Southern homes.

John, a Savannahian born and raised, bought Delta while living in London. "The main house, the old barn, the roaming wildlife . . . everything about Delta seemed to be built on rich Southern stories." The house lies on the front end of acres and acres of luscious Low Country land; the front of the property is speckled with rice fields. "We grow Carolina Gold here," John explains. "The seed was brought to the Carolinas from Madagascar in the early nineteenth century, and soon it was shipped all over the world." Until Sherman marched through, that is. But just a few years ago, the owner of Turnbridge, a neighboring plantation, revived the seed, and today, both plantations reap this Carolina Gold. Rice fields, however, are merely a side show.

Delta Plantation is primarily a hunting lodge—a comfortable, understated retreat, complete with a mud-room, gun room, gracious living and dining rooms, and cinema (for more modern retreaters) packed with a

ABOVE: Soft light pouring through French doors illuminates the wood-paneled living room. The painting over the mantel is by the Scottish artist Grouse Moore. On the table rests one of John's many wildlife bronzes and telescopes once used to spot stag in the distance while hunting on horseback.

library of favorite films. Visitors to Delta are greeted with a piercing stare from a mounted mahogany boar in the entranceway. "I remember wandering around Portobello Road early one morning right after I had purchased Delta, thinking, 'Delta needs an emblem, a coat of arms.' And as if by fate, I locked eyes with a mahogany boar." Boar, he explains, are indigenous to the area and continue to roam the plantation grounds. In fact, a note written

RIGHT: The strong, Gothic design of twin headboards in a guest bedroom contrasts perfectly with the delicate hand-painted lowboy and candlestick lamps. Sheer fabric panels hung from the ceiling, cool color on the walls, and simple, white matelassé create a serene, relaxing, almost monastic environment.

BELOW: Floral chintz, antique botanicals, sea grass carpeting, and bleached wood paneling lend the feel of an English manor house. A Christopher Murphy oil hangs above the bed inherited from John Cay's grandfather Hilton.

ABOVE LEFT: The entrance hall is alive with the thrill of the hunt, the warmth of the South, and the riches of genteel, family traditions. The carving of the wild boar over the doorway introduces the emblem of Delta Plantation.

ABOVE RIGHT: Antique decoys seem to take flight across the walls of Cay's office.

RIGHT: Morning light radiates through three French doors into the morning room. Ferns preserved by a nineteenth-century naturalist adorn walls covered with natural grass cloth. Taxidermic ducks form the centerpiece of this farmhouse table.

OVERLEAF: A round mahogany table creates an unpretentious dining experience and fosters easy conversation. Chairs are slipcovered in natural linen, embroidered with Delta's boar's head crest. The Peter Howell painting over the nineteenth-century English sideboard depicts a stretch of Saratoga where Cay occasionally races his horses.

on Delta stationery that sits on the ledge of a powder room window reads: "No need to close the blinds. There's no one but the boar outside." Comforting? I'm not sure. Today, however, the regal boar emblem pervades the entire home—from stationery to Carolina Gold packaging to dining room chair embroidery.

One could wander for days around John's home, enveloped in his stunning collection of wildlife art, antique hunting paraphernalia, and antique silver. Everything's arranged with a sophisticated, masculine touch confirming that a flair for gentlemanly pursuits remains alive and well. The colors are cool and natural, reflecting the serene setting surrounding the home. A prized collection of antique duck decoys perches on tabletops and walls as if they've just flown in from the plantation grounds. Deep-set windows in the upstairs guest rooms provide a sense of luxury as they frame verdant panoramas. Terraced lawns are ideal for croquet and cocktails. Beautifully worn nineteenth-century British furniture fosters a relaxed elegance characteristic of an English country home. "Nothing is un-Southern about my Anglophilia," John explains. "The British populated this area—crafted our city plans, built our first homes. We can thank the English for our Southern gentility."

As I leave the home, I ask about a stack of antique silver calling card trays displayed in the entry hall. "Southerners love collecting silver, because it's less expensive than gold . . . and we're poor in the South," John allows with a grin. Poor? The wildlife and history alone of Delta Plantation make John a very rich man, indeed. —*P.S.W.*

BELOW: French doors in the living room open onto acres of enchanting oasis.

Antique Silver

Antique silver has long been revered in the Southern home, owing to a strong affinity for both elegant entertaining and the handing down of valuable heirlooms. The classic silver serving set atop an old sideboard recalls the antebellum South, with its now mythic images of opulence and loyalty to the refinements of an English heritage.

Dawn E. Corley, also known as the "Charleston Silver Lady," says even early colonists of modest means sought to engrave a family crest or monogram on the precious metal to show ownership. In what seemed an untamed land, this distinguished a Southern family as part of civilized society. "Then as now, even the most casual setting achieves elevated status when silver is present," says Corley.

Indeed, when fortunes were lost, as during the Civil War, the family silver often symbolized the last possession of value from wealthier times. Stories abound of Southern women trying to hide valuables from Sherman's pillaging troops by burying the treasure in the yard or in the cemetery vault—perhaps beneath the very ancestors that first bestowed them.

In keeping with tradition, some children in the South are still given names that match the name or initials on silver from generations past, which they will someday inherit. And a young man may proudly carry his grandfather's silver flask, cigarette holder, or card case. Engraved items evoke one's ancestral lineage, always a cherished notion, but perhaps especially now when a sense of stability and roots can seem elusive.

In modern homes, antique silver can be used to make an original decorative statement with timeless appeal. A julep tumbler becomes a vase for an airy bunch of flowers, or an ornate compote might serve as a holder for vintage postcards or shells, showing off the Southern propensity for using priceless inherited gems in everyday ways. —*P.S.W.*

An intellectual yet unpretentious chic that flows from room to room.

ABOVE: Ann and David Silliman have filled their Victorian beach retreat with exquisite American Southern furniture and a soothing, family-friendly vibe.

OPPOSITE: Linen-slipcovered chairs are the perfect complement to this nineteenth-century trestle table simply adorned with three hurricane lamps. Hanging on the bead-board walls are a Confederate bond (right), and a stock certificate and dinner menu from the infamous *Titanic* voyage (left).

The Silliman House

Sullivan's Island, South Carolina

"In the afternoon they came unto a land / In which it seemed always afternoon," Alfred, Lord Tennyson wrote in his poem "The Lotus-Eaters." And so it feels upon our arrival at the weekend home of Ann and David Silliman—a nineteenth-century gem on Sullivan's Island, where lounging away languid afternoons (on a daybed suspended from the porch, no less) is a treasured pastime for the entire family.

The strong and storied Victorian bones of the home convey a rich narrative. Built in 1898—ironically enough, the same year that Ann's grandmother Ivy Patricia Morris was born—it was named Melrose by the original owner, a military officer stationed on the island. "I always wanted to rename the house Ivy Cottage, after my grandmother," Ann explains, "but for the sake of the kids, the Weekender works just fine."

Three dramatic white gables crowned with finials are juxtaposed against the cool blue of the awnings and cupolas, a color that Ann matched from a Tiffany's box. A large porch wraps around the gingerbread-style house with French doors leading into the living room, kitchen, and bedrooms. "Just looking at the porch," Ann exclaims, "makes you want to grab a mint julep and spend the entire day outside." While the approach to the home casts a comforting spell, it is but an allusion to the crisp and soothing ambience that awaits us inside.

Ann and David carved four bedrooms and four bathrooms out of the original three-bedroom, one-bath design. And, in the process, they've remained impeccably true to the integrity of the home. "If you just happen

ABOVE: Stark white makes a dramatic yet soothing statement in this "less is more" beach house kitchen.

LEFT: The pool house, which is original to the home, is surrounded by pecan trees; they rain copious amounts of nutty delights that the Silliman children love to gather.

OPPOSITE: The living room is illuminated with brilliant island light pouring in from the large windows and French doors that frame the room—the light bounces off the white walls and highlights the dark tones of the nineteenth-century American Southern furniture. The simplicity of this tablescape is personalized with vestiges of summers on Harbour Island and black-and-white family photos framed in antique silver.

to glance down at the wood floor, you can see the dirt and the lattice that lies beneath," Ann says. "We don't see it as poor insulation—these cracks add character and charm perfect for a family beach house." There's no question: the unpredictable island climate, the patina of age, and the daily sanding by active children and a well-loved dog have given this home personality and livability galore.

Finding the perfect pieces to adorn this Silliman slice of island paradise was not at all a chore for Ann and David—they're in the business of collecting. Over the past decade, they've grown a prosperous antiques business in Charleston, A. Fairfax Antiques, specializing in early-nineteenth-century American Southern furniture. So, when fashioning the perfect weekend home for their young family, the couple opted for "a clean, uncluttered look that not only showcased a collection of period Southern furniture but that also fostered the casual, easy-on-children lifestyle" that they adore.

But what's so unique about this home is that the atmosphere is far from expected. There is no sense of museumesque sterility, despite the museum quality of the pieces. There is no excess, no clutter, no need to add more to what speaks so eloquently on its own. A soothing serenity, a sense of renewal and contentment emanate from the breathing space surrounding each object. The bright white allows the rich mahogany to pop, while simultaneously inviting visitors to sit down and enjoy a peaceful refuge. The neutrals on the sofas, the natural linen on the dining room chairs, the hurricane lamps centered on the dining room table, the zebra rug, widespread family pictures, and the crisp, clean kitchen (where the blue floor matches the color of the pool's water, just outside the kitchen door) are the basis of an

intellectual yet unpretentious chic that flows from room to room. Their inspiration? The cool and comforting interiors of Harbour Island homes in the Bahamas—"a bucolic spot where Ann spent much of her childhood," David explains, and a place where this charming couple used to own property. "Alas, no more!"

"We often see passersby standing at the edge of our front porch, glancing through our habitually open front door into the center hall that leads straight through to the fireplace in the living room," Ann says. The hall is lined with a pleasant crowd of books, lending a cottage-y feel. "But the great thing is, the high ceilings and white walls add an unexpected dimension to the space." And should any of these curious onlookers step inside, or merely stretch out on the porch, they too would experience the pleasures of the perennial languid afternoon . . . hopefully, with a frosted mint julep in hand. —*P.S.W.*

ABOVE: Walls of books transform an expansive center hall into a warm and inviting environment.

RIGHT: Bright white bead board in the master bathroom exudes a feeling of clean. A collection of coral from Harbour Island in the Bahamas is tucked behind a stack of towels.

OPPOSITE: Crisp, cool, comfortable, and soothing, this screened-in front porch provides the perfect atmosphere for long chats and lemonade. Two beds hang on opposite ends from the haint blue ceiling just outside the bedroom doors. "Haint" is Low Country dialect for "haunt," and here refers to the shade of blue paint used to ward off evil spirits.

Southerners' houses

are nothing

if not evocative.

Cashiers, North Carolina

ABOVE: Newly constructed to look not so new, this house in the mountains of North Carolina, with its poplar bark shingles, six-over-one windows, high ceilings, and big porch, harkens back to Caroline Simons Finnerty's childhood summers.

OPPOSITE: In a concession to contemporary lifestyles, the dining and living areas are combined. Atlanta designer Carolyn Malone worked with a palette of soft, warm colors and embroidered and woven fabrics to create a vintage feel with modern freshness.

While there is much about the South to romanticize—and justifiably so—a long, hot, hideously humid summer is not one of them (with apologies and respects to George Gershwin, Porgy and Bess, et alia). This is why since the early nineteenth century, when the thermometer headed for a hundred, Southerners who could travel headed for the hills. The seasonal itinerant inclinations of Southerners from the Low Country and other stultifying and mosquito-stricken regions initially were not just for a change of pace, however. The summertime migration originated for health reasons, to escape pesky insect-borne fevers and illnesses.

"Flat Rock was the traditional summer colony of Charlestonians," explains Charleston native Caroline Simons Finnerty about the small town in the North Carolina Blue Ridge mountains. "We'd spend June at Sullivan's Island and July and August in the mountains. Except for my great-uncle Sam Stoney [one of the Low Country's more colorful characters and himself an author of books about Southern houses]; he thought Flat Rock was too much of a cocktail party and preferred to rough it in the wilds of Cashiers." And though today much of those wilds have been tamed (and Cashiers can be right much of a cocktail party itself!), the Finnerty family chose to have a weekend house in Cashiers for its proximity to Atlanta, where they live, and for its views.

The house is newly constructed, but heaven forbid it look that way. "I wanted it to feel like my great-grandmother built it," says Finnerty, fondly recalling

childhood days at her great-grandmother's in Flat Rock, where Finnerty and her brothers and cousins roared around the old rambling Victorian house with its high ceilings, wide veranda, and cool sleeping porch. Like Great-grandmother Belle herself, the house was both practical and commodious. Southerners' houses are nothing if not evocative. "And that's what I wanted this house to bring back for my children—those memories of telling ghost stories on the porch, making shadow puppets on the walls, waiting at night for the fairies to come out and dance on the chestnut stumps . . ."

Enter Atlanta designer Carolyn Malone, whose Alabama upbringing put her right in sync with Finnerty's desire for new takes on old fashions. "To me a Southern home is intensely personal, and it's a feeling you have when you walk in the door," says Malone. "We want elegance and comfort, yes, but we like for things to look like they've been there a while not like we went out and purchased a whole new room."

With soft, warm colors, heart pine floors, iron beds, chenille bedspreads, and ancient wing chairs covered in crewel-worked linen, the pair achieved a congenial congruence with the architecture and its

ABOVE: Old iron beds with quilts and shams made from vintage French grain sacks transport this old-fashioned sleeping porch back to a simpler time and slower pace—as they're meant to do.

RIGHT: Finnerty found this unusual antique rattan-and-cane chaise on a buying trip to France.

OPPOSITE: In the master bedroom, vintage linens and a chenille-like spread, from fabric Malone had made in India, dress a spool bed made by Ray Goins.

ABOVE AND RIGHT: Malone and Finnerty fashioned a European-style kitchen with Southern touches—and grits in the pantry. A French provincial server is pressed into service as a hardworking kitchen island, and a toile-lined, lattice-fronted cabinet offers storage with a dash of style.

nostalgic inclinations. Six-over-one windows frame the views. Transoms above the doors encourage the breezes. Pine plank paneling, poplar bark shingles, and even a sleeping porch complete the picture.

The children, too, are doing their part to re-create their mama's memories for themselves, albeit with at least one notable new addition: the youngest child (age ten at this writing) has established the exclusive "Club 207," named for the blueprint number of the odd, tiny room off the child's bedroom. Membership, though reportedly highly sought after by adults, is firmly denied to those over the age of twelve. Pity.

Pipsqueak impresarios aside, however, the house embraces a spirit of the past while accommodating realities of the present. For example, "In the old houses there would always have been a formal dining room," Finnerty acknowledges, "but we put the dining table in the living room instead."

Great-grandmother Belle would likely approve of it all—except, perhaps, for the name. The Finnertys call the house Bellewood, to which its provenance might have objected. "She would never let anyone be named after her, because she said the only other Belles she knew were either cows or madams," Finnerty says. "So now she finally has something named after her." Wonder what "Bellewood" would say? —*F.S.*

LEFT: This charming old zinc tub was found on a buying trip to France. A boudoir chair is covered in the same fabric as the master bed's coverlet.

OPPOSITE: The waterfall view is as pretty as a postcard.

It's

all about

"Come on in."

The Myers Park House

Charlotte, North Carolina

ABOVE: In keeping with the 1920s modernist spirit in which this Myers Park house in Charlotte was presumably built, the current owners added a wing for a new kitchen and family room, and put in an architecturally appropriate pool. The Taconic series chair, lounges, and dining set in the background are from Munder-Skiles in New York.

OPPOSITE: A ceramic "Foo" cat by North Carolina artist Betsy Towns watches over a pair of Ward Bennett "scissor chairs" (left), a Charles McMurray bench, and Hinson floor lamps.

Though architecture and interior design may offer clues to a house's provenance, they do not tell the entire story. And for those who think Southern houses are all about white columns and rocking chairs, this Texan-cum–Tar Heel owner might beg to differ. "To me what makes a house Southern is its sense of openness and graciousness," she begins. "Not to put the North down, but to me that usually is a distinction. I think of a Southern house as gracious." For hers in particular, a house in Charlotte's Myers Park she shares with her husband and three children, a feeling of welcome is implicit in the house's ample front porch and informal seating areas. "It's all about 'Come on in,'" she says. "At least I hope it is. That's how we feel about it."

The setting, too, is inviting, she says. "Everywhere you look are trees." Prestigiously located adjacent to the fabled Duke family estate, the neighborhood was planned at the turn of the century. The abundance of trees is thanks to a parcel of land between streets that was left undeveloped and designated as Edgehill Park. Though it was never laid out as a formal park, she points out, leaving an area "wild" was a device Frederick Law Olmsted used often in his work and which was fortunately broadly imitated. "So when we look out the front windows we see green instead of other houses."

Perhaps the suburban pastoral setting evokes some primal Southern yearning for days of rural yore, where the next farm or plantation may have been a several-hours' ride away. "And you didn't just come have tea in the parlor and leave," she says, "you stayed the night.

When you had company in your home, they were living there." Bane or blessing, "having company" was a Southern way of life, and custom compelled making one's home inviting.

It wasn't about showing off so much as it was about showing who you were. This really hasn't changed. While we were all taught by our mothers and grandmothers to be proper and decorus, she says, "Those of us who grew up in a Southern home grew up thinking we were supposed to put our personality out there, in the way we act, how we dress, and definitely in how we do our houses." Which doesn't mean doing things like everybody else.

"In a town filled with Georgian and redbrick Colonials, our house is very different," the young homeowner explains. When the couple bought the house several years ago, they were impressed with its eleven-foot ceilings and well-proportioned rooms. And though a second story had been added, along with columns on the front porch, the aim was to restore the house as much as possible to its original 1920s roots (and of course anything to do with roots is automatically Southern). The house most likely was built as "a little modernist bungalow," and much of it was intact. The porte cochere was original, with its massive squared-off columns; and the materials used—stucco, plaster, and terrazzo, with little or no decoration—all pointed in what at the time would have been a modernist direction.

This belle may be departing from the standard notion of "traditional Southern," but she nevertheless remains steadfastly true to her Southern heritage. "I grew up in a house quite mixed," she says. "We had antique furniture and chintz, but there was always a lot of other stuff mixed in. And my aunt has a very modern house, with a lot of original

ABOVE: In the living room, Donghia chairs combine effortlessly with Knoll classics, a small Warren Platner table, and the black marble-topped round table from Saarinen. Gracing the Platner table is an Elsa Peretti "Thumbprint" bowl, and "A Gaggle of Gourds" by late Carolina artist Clara Couch nests atop the Saarinen. The gaggle was formerly tended to by the husband's late mother.

OPPOSITE: In the hallway looking toward the living room are early Windsor chairs from Christies New York, where the wife used to work. A portrait of the husband's grandmother keeps an eye on things.

Knoll furniture, so I did understand that sensibility." Fortunately, her husband shared it.

With the help of former Bud Oglesby protégé Kathleen Munoz from Dallas, the family went about furnishing their house with select modernist pieces, a black marble Saarinen table here, a Charles McMurray bench there, all seeming happily to coexist with the "brown furniture" handed down from their respective families. The art and objects are decidedly modern, their budding collection highlighted by many works of North Carolina artists, including all three generations of the Jugtown Pottery family, the Owens. Her Sheraton-style dining room table, often topped by a colorful contemporary glass bowl, is surrounded by mid-century modern T.H. Robsjohn-Gibbings chairs. A giant ceramic "Foo" cat sometimes stands guard by the fireplace. "Nothing is very set; I have some unexpected things, too—it's sorta quirky." Like a Southern house is sorta supposed to be.

When the time came to add a new kitchen and informal dining and seating area, the couple turned to the Dallas design team of Bodron+Fruit, working closely with Mil Bodron to achieve a look that was modern yet warm and, well, gracious. There's that word again. Thank goodness. —*F.S.*

RIGHT: A wedding gift from the bride's mother, a pair of antique silver wine coolers takes tulips and pride of place on the living room mantel.

OPPOSITE: The current owners added a new kitchen and "living porch" in total keeping with their modern aesthetic and yet appropriate to the period of the house and its Southern context. The La Paloma stools are from Conran's; the light fixtures are by Artemide.

People say they're so glad I'm keeping the history of the house . . .

The Capel House

Chapel Hill, North Carolina

ABOVE: On a shady sidewalk behind a picket fence, this cheerful clapboard bungalow was built in 1936 as a father's wedding gift to his daughter, champion golfer Estelle Lawson Page. Current owner Mary Clara Capel has restored the original lattice design for the entry.

OPPOSITE: On the sunny screened porch, early spring branches flower above an old farm table from Montgomery County, North Carolina. The decorative chair is cast aluminum bought at Capel's seventh-grade English teacher's estate auction.

On a leafy side street in the storied college town of Chapel Hill, North Carolina, home of the nation's oldest state university, is "the Page House." The Pages don't live there now, mind you, but it will always be the Page House, says current owner Mary Clara Capel. "It's not the Capel house. It'll never be the Capel house." That's a funny thing about Southern houses; people become attached to them even if they don't belong to them. They become attached to a house as a part of their own history—to how the house and its inhabitants were part of the town they grew up in, the community they shared; to a house where their own family or friends might have called, or trick-or-treated, or sung Christmas carols. Mary Clara takes no exception; she is a Southerner, too.

And this particular house does have a history worth preserving. It was built in 1936 as a wedding gift to Estelle Lawson and her new husband, Julius Page, from her father, a physician affiliated with the university's medical school and also the university's first athletic director. Daddy didn't want his daughter to be a doctor, so she turned to golf and in 1937 won the U.S. Women's Amateur. She went on to compete professionally all over the country and was one of the first members of the North Carolina Sports Hall of Fame.

"My office was her trophy room," says Mary Clara "with a b-i-i-i-g glass case packed with silver and the walls covered in memorabilia." Mary Clara bought what she could from the estate sale, including "a fabulous soup tureen that was the runner-up prize from a tournament

ABOVE LEFT: "Everybody loves the porch best," says Capel. "It's just off the kitchen so it makes it easy to have big outdoor dinner parties." The made-to-order swing by SFK Furniture in Troy copies the lattice detail of the porch panels and the front entrance.

ABOVE RIGHT: A collection of funky folk art made by the Alabama Folk Art Company gathers in the far back corner garden. The bird in the tree is a chain-saw carving from the North Carolina mountains. Capel painted it to look like a blue bird.

LEFT: Bright yellow forsythia perks up an old tin pot, part of Capel's collection of graniteware. Other pieces are hung on the side of the garden house in back.

OPPOSITE: A cutout in the gate lets passersby see into the pretty Mac Newsom–designed garden. The large, strap hinges were custom made by Newbern Douglas, of Sophia, North Carolina.

in Texas. I'd hate to see what the winner got." For practical reasons Mary Clara had to dispense with the glass case, but she has dedicated an "Estelle wall" to the memory of her predecessor and generally has honored the spirit of the house as the modest but charming bungalow that it is. "People say they're so glad I'm keeping the history of the house and not trying to make it something it wasn't."

And yet Mary Clara has made her mark on the house. A creative spirit and practiced painter, Mary Clara is the director of administration of Troy-based Capel Rugs, founded in 1917 by her grandfather, who went from making plow lines to braiding rugs. Mary Clara has very clear notions about what makes a Southern house a Southern home, and, surprise, it's all about the kitchen and the porch. She put in a great kitchen, "that people can hang out in while I cook," she says, "but everybody's favorite spot is the screened porch. It's got a real high ceiling and a big, deep swing done in the Cumberland Island style so you can curl up in there and take a nap." Latticework over part of the screening creates privacy without impeding the light.

Elsewhere Mary Clara has put her own glam-ish spin on the casual cottage style, and lavished care on her garden and guest cottage—the former to funk it up with folk art and eccentric birdhouses; the latter to double as a painting studio. She's also fashioned a comfy outdoor living room on a brick terrace, furnished with old-timey painted metal chairs and a genuine "glider," of a sofa, like you just don't see much anymore.

"It's definitely got my touches," she says, "but I'd like to think the Pages would be happy with what I've done." —F.S.

ABOVE: The "memory wall" Capel has created honoring her famous predecessor in the house. The "Spade" chair was originally made for a set of casino chairs and is covered in Fortuny fabric Capel picked up in Venice.

LEFT: A collection of old seltzer bottles rests on the dining room table. The corner cupboard holds a collection of, from top, old silver, a hand-carved swan decoy, North Carolina crystalline glazed pottery, silver christening and trophy cups, and china. The chandelier is by Currey and Company.

OPPOSITE: Capel is a consummate hostess and had the old kitchen remodeled for both cooking and company. Architect Jack Haggerty from Carrboro assured her she would like it, as he was a former chef. "He was right!" she says.

The house was All About Eve in a neighborhood that was more about Leave It to Beaver.

ABOVE: Architects Bobby McAlpine and Ken Pursley worked with Posie Mealy to adapt this third-generation family house to modern family living. The fixtures and decorative iron storm door are original to the house.

OPPOSITE: Key to the design was an addition connecting the original house to the garage, which was renovated as living quarters. The new structure, with its striking wall of steel-cased windows, surrounds a courtyard.

The Mealy House

Charlotte, North Carolina

"I spent every year of my life coming to this house," says Posie Patrick Mealy. At one time both her grandparents and parents lived here, so it is where she spent every holiday. Mealy herself lives here now, with her husband, Mark, and three children, hoping that one day one of them might carry on. "Nothing would make me happier," she says. Even in the South, where family traditions hold tight, the successive generational home has become an anomaly. But then this house is somewhat of an anomaly itself.

Built in 1935 by a prominent Charlotte family in the transportation business, the house was and is in an art deco Mediterranean style—definitely more Hollywood than Mecklenburg County. With a stucco exterior, marble floors, a spiral staircase, and steel-casement windows, the house was *All About Eve* in a neighborhood that was more about *Leave It to Beaver*.

All systems were state-of-the-art. It was the first house in town—and maybe the state—to have central air-conditioning. "It had an electrical panel that could juice the entire neighborhood," Mealy says, adding somewhat sheepishly, if humorously, that there might have been a tile roof, but building codes at the time forbade "Mexican" houses. (Thankfully, this part of the code, like other shall we say less-than-enlightened ethnic references, have long been purged from Southern cities' official specifications, building and otherwise.) People could scarcely afford to build that way in 1935; but even if they could, who knew how? Industrial builders, that's who, and they are who constructed the house to

commercial specifications—and for a very particular way of living.

With only three bedrooms, large public rooms, and a small, isolated kitchen, the house was contrived for a rather glamorous, grown-up lifestyle more suited to formal entertaining and occasional houseguests than to casual gatherings and boisterous resident families. When the Mealys decided to move in, they knew they would need creative solutions, and fortunately they knew whom to ask.

Though he doesn't really do "renovations" anymore, preeminent Alabama architect and Tar Heel transplant Bobby McAlpine was intrigued by the project and endeared to the clients, having completed a beach house for them several years earlier. So McAlpine and project architect Ken Pursley, who has since struck out on his own, took it on.

The challenge from a design standpoint was how to reconcile the "old South" idea of a third-generation home with this slightly kooky, modern, 1930s deco-glam thing. "I didn't want to traditionalize it," McAlpine begins. "What we wanted to do was make it a better one of what it was. What was modern, make more modern. What was sexy, make more so." They also wanted to play up the Mediterranean aspect of the house.

All design directives were accomplished in the deft stroke of a central courtyard, surrounded by the garage converted to a family-friendly wing linked to the original house by a new kitchen and an informal dining area that look out onto the courtyard through a wall of windows. The windows match those original to the house, steel-cased and custom fabricated—an extravagance Mealy appreciates fully now in retrospect. And the courtyard, Mealy says, "is the most beautiful room in the

house," with the new kitchen serving as "the heart and soul" of this new, old home. Instead of putting in a big kitchen island, they brought in a nine-foot trestle table. And with no overhead cabinets the room "doesn't feel like a kitchen," she says, "and we love it." Likewise, the adjacent dining alcove, which perfectly seats five but is cozy enough for three, is just right for the Mealy family and their children's various stages.

An experienced decorator herself, like her mother, Rose Patrick, before her, Mealy sought the help of McAlpine and partner-designer Ray Booth

OPPOSITE: Mealy didn't want the kitchen to "feel like a kitchen," and with the help of interior designer Ray Booth managed to create a beautiful room that is also fully functional. Open shelving replaces overhead cabinets; the floors and countertops are concrete; and the walls are stucco.

BELOW: A butler's pantry offers more storage and an inviting informal dining nook as viewed from the entrance hall. Booth designed the curving built-in banquette, a signature McAlpine-Booth element. The table is nineteenth-century Italian. The iron light fixtures on both pages are from Dennis & Leen.

for her new interiors. The collaboration proved to be an editing process that she says pushed her into a "more clean, contemporary look than I might have done on my own." Once-favored prints and chintzes are forgone for textured linens and cottons, monotonal damasks, and softly worn leathers. French and Italian antiques nose in on formerly English territory. In a palette of warm neutrals and muted hues, rooms overall are pared down and decluttered, allowing visual space for the pieces remaining to be fully appreciated.

The result is a house that works both as a gracious home for family and a superb venue for entertaining—which the Mealys do, often and well. The very character of the place that compelled its transformation ultimately kept it true to its Southern soul and its eccentric self. By designing a house that embraces its past as well as its present, Mealy hopes also to presage the family home's future as it passes into the hands of the next generation. It would be so satisfying, and so wonderfully Southern, too. —*F.S.*

LEFT: The original curving marble stair and iron-and-brass banister make a glamorous entrance and chic perch for a late-eighteenth-century Italian grotto bench, a gift from Posie's parents.

OPPOSITE: A beautiful eighteenth-century French barometer from Caroline Faison Antiques in Greensboro, North Carolina, hangs in front of a sunny living room window looking onto the interior courtyard. The table is nineteenth-century Italian gilt and marble. The chinoiserie box was purchased on a trip to Hong Kong.

It feels like you are floating on a sea of green and looking out over the water.

The Groom House

Clairborne, Maryland

If I could write only one sentence about this house, that sentence would be: Mineral Spring Farm, the Eastern Shore home of the inimitable Ruth Noble ("Baba") Groom, has many beguiling features, but perhaps the most intriguing is the poetry shed.

Fortunately, space permits a few more sentences. But you know how sometimes you can just know one or two things about a person or a place and suddenly you know a lot more than that? A restaurant, for instance, that keeps the ketchup and Tabasco sauce bottles right there on the table. Or a great-aunt who painted her nails bright pink and had her poodle dyed to match. You know what I mean. To me the poetry shed at Baba Groom's is that kind of telling detail. But the poetry shed, which I'll come back to, is only the beginning.

"It's just an old farmhouse," Groom begins, "and I thought it looked lonely sitting at the end of that drive-way. The house isn't particularly historic, and for the Eastern Shore it's not real significant except that you don't find this kind of house much up here." In the storied enclave that is Maryland and Virginia's intricately carved Chesapeake coastline, many of the old houses reflect the early-nineteenth-century trend toward more austere Federal architecture. Groom's house, however, built circa 1860, is more approachably Victorian. "It's one of those wonderful old porch-y houses like you get in the South," she says. Standing as it does on a slight knoll above a small, beckoning bay, "It feels like you are floating on a sea of green and looking out over the water. That's what enchanted me."

ABOVE: Baba Groom thought this old farmhouse looked lonely at the end of its long, straight drive, but it's had plenty of company since then.

OPPOSITE: From the peak-ceiling foyer to the living room, a tall vase brims with willow branches towering above Japanese magnolia blossoms and an iron candlestick on a Sheraton-style table.

Groom, who was married to writer Winston Groom (author of *Forrest Gump*) and then to businessman Dan Wallace, now deceased, currently shares the house with nearest and dearest companions, friends, and creatures, the last including Welleran Poltarnees, a 205-pound English mastiff, and cats Clara, Thelma, and Louise.

"Anyway, it's a barefoot summer kind of house," she says, "the kind where you wake up whenever you want and for lunch you have tomato sandwiches and Coca-Colas." Groom acquired the house in 1990, when married to Wallace, who died seven years later. (Wallace, incidentally, was the larger-than-life inspiration for his novelist son Daniel Wallace's acclaimed 1998 novel *Big Fish,* also a hit feature film.) But they bought the farm less for the house than they did for the land, Groom says. "Southerners are particularly in tune with the idea of home and land. It's terribly important about the soil the house sits on and the

way the trees relate to the house. Most Southern architecture looks outward, not inward, and it's been that way *forevah*." For the rural house in particular, be it humble shotgun shack or Greek Revival manse, the porch is essential.

If Southern hospitality begins at home, it enters by the porch, which is a welcome in itself. "You're already under the eaves when you ring the bell, so the house kind of embraces you," says the gracious hostess, whose own incomparable brand of hospitality reflects her thoughts of home. "Originally we were a cordial people making our way in a pretty raw land," she explains, "but I have a friend who says it's important to remember that Massachusetts was settled by *Puritans,* and Virginia was settled by *Cava-lee-ahs.* I think in the South there is more of an emphasis on being fun." (Safe for me to say, by the way, that Groom knows whereof she speaks.)

Groom, who also lives in Washington, D.C., does most of her weekend entertaining here. "You are encouraged if you are a guest to be amusing," she says. But the guest's obligation to be entertaining is equal to that of the hostess's to entertain. Groom makes it easy, though, by supplying her guests with great material. Included in her weekend agendas are strolls at dusk to have cocktails with the horses and evening roundups of the resident peacocks. There might be a visit to the small and fastidiously

LEFT: The view from the back porch, across the terrace, to a tranquil, sheltered bay of the Chesapeake. Red, the resident Appaloosa, and Buddy, the burro, graze contentedly.

OPPOSITE: "It's one of those wonderful old porch-y houses like you get in the South," Groom says. The Chinese Chippendale-style bench was created at the farm.

ABOVE LEFT: A second-story gazebo offers a clear view of the water and is an inviting alfresco bedroom.

ABOVE RIGHT: Groom rings the bell by the front door to summon cats and dogs to dine.

LEFT: For cigars and brandy after dinner, reciting verse and otherwise holding forth, Groom's famous "poetry shed" is fashioned from an old tobacco barn and furnished with a motley collection of furnishings that serves its purpose just fine.

Or they may be invited to snooze in Groom's outdoor bedroom gazebo.

All charming Southern houses "have a little surprise somewhere," Groom says. And while the houses may be graceful and elegant, they also have soft edges. The South likely has taken its cue from English country houses that way, she says. "We don't have our silver too highly polished and don't mind scratches on the furniture. Things are old and not perfect, and we like them that way." Better poetry than perfection, any day. —*F.S.*

ABOVE LEFT: A wooden hawk watches over the sunny mudroom, which is furnished with an old pie safe and a church pew bench. The musical frog was a gift from a friend. The painted trunk at bottom left is an old sea chest.

ABOVE: Canvas curtains tied to wire cables work as room dividers in a refurbished barn-become-guesthouse. In the background is a small flying pig.

maintained cemetery, which contains the graves of the early-eighteenth-century inhabitants of Mineral Spring Farm, Groom's late husband Wallace, two cherished friends, and a menagerie of beloved and sundry critters and pets. An impressive bronze sculpture of an osprey guards the souls resting there. Such family burial grounds are common to rural Southern houses. After dinner, guests may be invited to the poetry shed, a tiny converted tobacco barn with ersatz seating, a rather dusty set of shelves for tattered tomes of verse, and an odd mixture of lanterns and flashlights to read by. "I usually have a box of cigars out there, and some brandy—or bourbon. It is always an adventure, and people love to read!"

Upon retiring some guests may amble off to the nearby guesthouse, a (sort of) renovated old barn that has the kitchen on the front porch. "In case it rains," says Groom, "it's an alternative for a picnic."

We Southerners are far less provincial than the Yankees would have you believe . . .

ABOVE: Inspired by his clients' love of British country houses, architect Lewis Graeber III designed a classic Georgian manse in Jackson, Mississippi.

OPPOSITE: The consummate hostess, Mollie VanDevender can configure her dining room to seat up to twenty-four using the large round table and corner banquettes. The enormous window frames a garden view set off beautifully by the room's deep chocolate walls.

The VanDevender House
Jackson, Mississippi

"I read years ago—I can't remember where—a quotation I liked so much I wrote it on a card and set it in a place card holder on a table in the living room. It went something like 'Contrary to popular belief, we Southerners are far less provincial than the Yankees would have you believe. I mean how many Yankees would you catch moving to Alabama or Mississippi for a few years? We understand the North, we've lived up there . . .' And it's the truth!" So begins the conversation with Alabama-bred, New York–based designer Richard Keith Langham about Mollie and Billy VanDevender's house in Jackson, Mississippi. "Their house's décor is gleaned from all over the world," he says, a fact clearly signaled from the moment of entry into a circular foyer whose limestone floor is inlaid with a compass rose and whose walls portray murals of four continents.

As much as that rotunda reflects the cosmopolitan inclinations of its inhabitants, however, it also announces the American South. Mississippi Delta–born architect Lewis Graeber III positioned at the end of the living room, on axis with the front door, a large Palladian-style window that frames a view of the garden so inviting you want to walk right into it. Truly, says Graeber, "This house could be anywhere in the world." But for the setting, says the chatelaine. "As I sit here I am looking out at all the azaleas; and the dogwoods are blooming; the magnolias are out."

It is a theme that recurs constantly in relation to Southern homes: this connection to nature, to the environment, and to the earth. And as Southern houses

almost invariably relate to the outdoors, quite often so do Southerners themselves, in a way that harkens back to their earliest forebears. Learning to hunt and fish remains a rite of passage for many a young Southern son and, occasionally, a Southern daughter as well. Whether tracking antelope in Africa or shooting quail close to home, Mollie VanDevender feels a closeness to the land she and her kin have known for generations. "It's in my blood," she says—and it is a family thing. "I'd rather be hunting with my children than for them." Amen to that, sister.

About her house she says, not surprisingly, that she wanted a comfortable home for her family, which includes four very active children. "I wanted something warm and livable but also eye-pleasing and elegant," she says (something a former Miss Mississippi should know about), "and I really believe we achieved that."

That she, Graeber, and Langham are all Southerners, Langham says, allowed for their mutual understanding of an implicit cultural vernacular "that was there from the get-go. And the pieces fell into place because of that."

Inspired by travel and an affinity for Georgian architecture—country houses in particular—VanDevender loves that "each room is unique, but as Keith says, they all hold hands." Indeed the airy, ice-cream-y living room leads to the moody, mulled wine-colored library; leads to the warm, chocolate brown dining room; leads to the endless

LEFT: Signaling the worldly inclinations of its well-traveled inhabitants, the rotunda's limestone floor is inlaid with a compass rose, and the four walls are hung with panels depicting Africa, Asia, Europe, and North America.

shades of green beyond the windows. The house is handsomely decorated with a kind of luxurious spareness that bespeaks impeccable choices in furnishings and fabrics and exquisitely honed collections—from luminous Irish Belleek porcelain to rough, glinting geodes to glowering big-game trophies. The rooms and their contents offer one "tantalizing vista" after another, Langham says, that "embraces the grand without becoming pretentious."

The same might be said of VanDevender's near-legendary entertaining style. "I still like good old-fashioned Southern dinner parties," she says. "That's why I have my dining room the way it is. With the round table and two corner banquettes I can bring in extra chairs and seat twenty-four. It seems like a lot but it really is cozy."

Family meals are taken in the dining room as well. "I know people are doing away with that these days," she says, but she was brought up that way and deems it important to continue. Naught to do with fine china, polished silver, or starched linen (though that's all very nice), true Southern hospitality is what Southerners do every day. A house like the VanDevenders', with its worldly elegance and rich charms, may dispel a stereotype or two about living in the South; but it seems the people living in it are perpetuating another: how they treat their own at home and how they treat other folks out in the world. "It's the way we reach out," VanDevender says, recalling the outpouring of help and support for their Gulf Coast neighbors after Hurricane Katrina. "They were not looking for accolades; it's just the way they've been raised." Having been 'round the world and back again, "That's what I know and what I see." —F.S.

ABOVE: Langham designed a pair of banquettes to allow the hostess to seat up to twenty-four guests in the dining room. The plates are from her collection. Flat-finish chocolate walls set off the glow of gilded sconces.

OPPOSITE: Designer Richard Keith Langham calls the library color "mulled wine." With its leather wing chair, tartan upholstery, stag antler chandelier, and Grinling Gibbons–style carving, the room could have come straight from a hunting lodge in Scotland.

LEFT: A zebra trophy obliges the black-and-white scheme of the garden room, tented to resemble safari-style lodging. The upholstered metal furnishings were designed by Langham.

OPPOSITE: In the tradition of eighteenth- and nineteenth-century English country houses and grounds, Graeber designed a classical garden folly and formal garden. The glass-domed pavilion also serves as the guesthouse. Behind it is a green-house, where the VanDevenders have held dances.

A tidal wave of color

and texture pulls visitors

deep into this uptown

pocket of whimsy . . .

ABOVE: Some of the Crescent City's most cherished visual treats are its unique residences, like this shotgun-style house that flourished in turn-of-the-century New Orleans. Long and narrow, the shotgun houses combined Caribbean and Haitian house designs.

OPPOSITE: With a riot of bright colors and a mélange of textures, Mary Bigelow creates a living room environment that reflects her own joie de vivre. Rather than heavy drapery, vertical lines of artwork frame large windows that illuminate the room with bright Louisiana light.

The
Bigelow House
New Orleans, Louisiana

From Flannery O'Connor to Tennessee Williams, Southern literati have woven colorful tales around an assortment of eccentrics. For, unlike other regions of the country, the South seems to elevate its unconventional denizens to regal heights. In a quiet neighborhood tucked behind Tulane University, we find the home of Mary Ferry Bigelow—a capricious New Orleanian who seems to have escaped from the pages of a Southern novel. Her house, the evocative illustrations that accompany the text.

Mary was born and raised in this house and, after living all over the country, returned to the streets of her childhood in 1986. From the outside, the home looks like a typical shotgun-style house that flourished in the Crescent City at the turn of the century. (As the legend goes, a bullet fired from the front door could exit the back door without destroying anything in its path. Ergo, a "shotgun" house.) But don't let the traditional architectural style indigenous to the area or the demure gray exterior fool you. Behind the pink door, a tidal wave of color and texture pulls visitors deep into this uptown pocket of whimsy—an interior that perfectly captures Mary's personality and reflects her characteristic New Orleans vim.

Right around the corner lives Mrs. Genevieve Trimble, one of Mary's early design mentors, to whom she credits her penchant for vibrant color. "I remember walking into her home and being enthralled by this glass vase filled with turquoise-colored water. The color reflected all over the room and matched her turquoise

kitchen as if she had contemplated it for hours. Of course, Mrs. Trimble still looks divine at . . . well, Southern ladies never reveal their age." That vision of turquoise has gone a long, long way, indeed. Today, Mary's entire home seems to place color—whether patterned, layered, or faux-finished—upon the highest pedestal.

Among the many marvelous vignettes in Mary's uptown bungalow, I can't take my eyes off a pile of gnarled tennis balls arranged almost like a contemporary sculpture beneath a coffee table in the living room. "Those nasty things?!" Mary exclaims in her high-pitched drawl. "Rosarie collects them. Each time we walk by the Tulane tennis courts, she brings another one home." Rosarie, named for Mary's love affair with Parisian rose gardens, is her standard poodle.

Like many steel magnolias of the South, Mary has definite opinions about her taste. Pink, purple, and turquoise—and lots of it—are the staples of her

ABOVE: In the dining room, raspberry walls add an unexpected punch of humor to an otherwise genteel setting. The precise arrangement of this set of nineteenth-century Pompeiian stage prints is an unexpected formal counterpoint to the jazzy interior.

LEFT: A busy table covered in chintz and German china sets the stage for a lively meal. The chairs, originally Mary's mother's, are faux malachite.

ABOVE: A sturdy collection of obelisks and Mexican porcelain plates with silver inlay grace this marble-top table designed by local artist Mario Valla.

RIGHT: Mary drenches her kitchen with watermelon pink. The 1940s O'Keefe and Merritt stove still turns out a tasty jambalaya. Jars to the right of the stove are filled with a lifetime's supply of dog biscuits.

home. "I try to 'de-white' my life," she explains. (Although describing her style, "de-whiting" comes across as oddly philosophical.) The first time I met Mary, I was struck by the fact that she actually blended in with her interiors: she wore black jeans and a turquoise shirt under a pink sweater. Later, as she rolled down the top to her Volkswagen convertible on the way to lunch, she tossed on her big purple sunglasses. Coincidence? Absolutely not. Everything about Mary—her dress, her laughter, her ability to talk for hours on end, and, indeed, her home—reflect her personality to a "B." Yes, Southern homes often feature high ceilings, intricate moldings, screened-in porches, and, lest we forget, well-stocked bars. But a true Southern home embraces a particular Southerner's Southern roots— with all the inherent idiosyncrasies.

"A cousin of mine says that I'm the 'eccentric' of the family," Mary claims with coquettish pride and a hearty laugh. For this New Orleans original, as long as her design de-whites, it's quite doubtful she'll be dethroned. —*P.S.W.*

LEFT: Even the powder room is exotic! A large-print foil wallpaper expands this small space into a fantastical niche with an iron table designed by New Orleans sculptor David Rochold.

OPPOSITE: The American Empire canopy bed and chest have been staples of this room since Mary's childhood. Framed portraits of Mary's Creole parents on the dresser are a reminder that this home is built on a strong foundation of rich Southern memories.

A visual feast—

with a helping of

anecdotes for dessert.

The
Ogden House

Roger Ogden is well known in Louisiana circles, as is the Ogden Museum of Southern Art in New Orleans, which he founded and to which he has donated the bulk of his extraordinary collection of nineteenth- and twentieth-century paintings, prints, photography, sculpture, crafts, and drawings. What may not be so well known, however, is the degree to which the real estate entrepreneur and self-taught art connoisseur is personally responsible for the revival of Southern art and artists and for their sustained popularity in today's ever-fickle art world. Like charity, appropriately, this story begins at home—a very Southern home.

"I acquired the house with the idea that it would be an appropriate venue for the art," Ogden says. The year was 1978 and his collecting was "in full mode," much like his then seven-year-old son, who needed the house's big yard to full-mode around in. Situated on one of the largest tracts in uptown New Orleans, the house encouraged boys to be boys and men to be collectors. And likewise the collection encouraged the house, as well as its furnishing and decoration, in a felicitous symbiosis with Ogden's finely honed and highly personal aesthetic.

Damaged but not defeated when Katrina roared through in 2005, the noble Greek Revival manse embodies the iconic architectural style so inexorably linked with the antebellum South. The classical portico and Corinthian columns, however, belie its original construction in 1890 as a more Victorian statement, heavily punctuated with the likes of turrets and bronze

ABOVE: Built in 1890 originally in the Eastlake style with some Italianate features, the Ogden manse in uptown New Orleans acquired its Greek Revival façade in a 1931 remodeling.

OPPOSITE: Arranged salon style in the grand foyer are selections from Roger Ogden's remarkable collection of Southern art. "The Carr Children" by William Henry Baker, circa 1855, hangs above an early-nineteenth-century Philadelphia settee. The floors of alternating walnut and white ash are original to the house.

ABOVE: In the billiard room are paintings
by Alexander Drysdale depicting New
Orleans's City Park. The custom pool table
by Golden West Billiards in California
rests on an antique Chinese rug.

RIGHT: Italian pheasants of shell and
silver plate perch along an eighteenth-
century George II breakfront containing
silver serving pieces. The Baccarat chandelier is original to house. The chairs are
late-eighteenth-century Chippendale.

OPPOSITE: In the drawing room, an
imposing Louis XIV–style chandelier
was made by Baccarat, circa 1860. The
George I lacquer cabinet (circa 1730)
holds a collection of fine blue-and-white
Chinese porcelain. The portrait on the
easel (artist unknown) is of Sam Houston,
Ogden's distant uncle. A pair of old leather
Chesterfield sofas and a contemporary
Lucite coffee table keep the room honest
and comfortable for everyday living.

sculptures. A renovation in 1931 produced the current façade, which acknowledges its past as well as
its present. The house's double stair and wrought-
iron balustrade bespeak Louisiana plantation style,
while arched and double-hung windows reflect
Italianate tendencies. "The beauty is, it works,"
says Ogden, "but it must have been a scary exercise
for the architects involved."

The interiors as well defy facile categorization.
"I get bored with pure period rooms," he says,
"They're fine for museums but not for living in."
That he prefers to mix periods and origins is
rather stating the obvious. With furnishings from
austere Federal to fussy French, and art from
Dominico Canova to Ida Kohlmeyer, the house's
commodiously proportioned rooms, with high-high

ceilings and hand-carved moldings, are nothing short of a visual feast—with a helping of anecdotes for dessert. *(Did you hear about the time Eugene McCarroll broke the arm of the dining room chandelier? That'll happen to a chandelier when you swing on it. Oh, and he's the only man ever to have been named king of Proteus—twice. . . .)*

And then there is The Collection itself, about which much has been and will be written, what with its Audubons, Drysdales, Rockmores, and Sullys. The dusting alone must require a small militia. Photographed in situ, perhaps for the last time for this book, some six hundred works of Ogden's collection will go to the museum as soon as their new home is ready: the Taylor library building, designed by the renowned nineteenth-century

architect H. H. Richardson and part of the museum complex. Ogden's recent munificence is in addition to the six hundred pieces he has already gifted the museum with since its founding in 2003.

Such splendid art and grand architecture understandably begs to be uptight, self-conscious—*Oh, don't sit on that!*—and yet, "No, it is not," Ogden confirms matter-of-factly. "We tried purposefully to retain the stately nature of the house's scale and design but to make it warm and inviting, and easy to live in." Southern. There was also, in the beginning, the matter of a seven-year-old on the loose. . . . "Besides, I like to live in eclectic surroundings. Maybe it reflects my personality—my love of sports and business and also my passion for arts and culture." The man's a veritable polymath.

Pulling together these various decorative schemes has been a "series of collaborations," he says, with the much-admired, late Tom Collum, Tony Masters and Doug Ballard, and lately with Louis Aubert. Those great old Chesterfield sofas in the drawing room are owing to Masters and Ballard; the Plexiglas table between them to Collum. The masterfully subtle shades of white on the exterior clapboard and the snappy upholstery in the solarium go to colorist and designer Aubert. The drawing room's elegant Fortuny curtains are thanks to Masters and Ballard. The media room's contemporary punch was thrown by Collum. But it was all Ogden in the end. "I didn't want a home that was 'decorated' but I did want it to be informed by design."

Informed by design and about to undergo dramatic transition. As the art that has adorned and defined it is swept away, Ogden's house presents parallels that are compelling. Like the culture that

ABOVE: In the library, a George III breakfront with Gothic tracery holds a collection of porcelain birds by Dorothy Doughty and Edward Marshall Boehm. The red boulle marquetry is Louis XIV.

RIGHT: One of the jewels of the collection, "Mother Louisiana" by Dominico Canova, hangs above a Joseph Meeks and Sons pier table (circa 1829). The Queen Anne–style chairs are nineteenth-century American. Above them hangs a pair of George Coulon watercolors.

OPPOSITE: A late-eighteenth-century George III drum table and pair of carved William & Mary chairs (circa 1700) occupy a corner.

fostered this great collection, and the city that proudly claims it, Ogden's house must reinvent itself to carry on, both for him and future generations. Though under far less grievous circumstances than the havoc of war or the ravages of nature, "It's a fact," Ogden states, "there is both the end of a chapter and the opportunity to begin a new one." At this trying time in its history, New Orleans is fortunate to have as advocate a man of such style and substance. —*F.S.*

ABOVE: Made in 1850 by C. Lee, a man of color, the massive mahogany four-poster bed is a replica of one in the Texas governor's mansion that was made for Ogden's ancestor Sam Houston. The zebra rug and elephant tusks are exotic touches.

OPPOSITE: In the rear courtyard, a circular staircase leads to the sundeck above the solarium and echoes the contours of "Continuum," by the contemporary American sculptor Lin Emery.

A French legacy and British élan can harmonize quite beautifully.

The Rowe House

Lafayette, Louisiana

ABOVE: A verdant brick courtyard and front porch welcome visitors into Rob and Tina Rowe's warm home, which was designed by renowned Louisiana architect A. Hays Town.

OPPOSITE: The wall of books—all slightly tattered with affection—adds an immeasurable sense of warmth to this living room nook; eighteenth-century French oils hung between the shelves provide visual pause. A collection of porcelain greyhounds on the mahogany tripod and needlepoint pillows on the sofa attest to the family's canine love affair.

Books in the dining room, books on the bedroom floor, books heaped on tables, stacked on footstools, and pyramidded on chairs within an arm's reach of . . . everything. "We're addicted readers in our family," Tina Rowe admits, "and displaying books throughout the home is just symptomatic of that addiction." The urge to grab several novels and curl up in a beckoning chair beside Harriet Beecher Rowe, one of the Rowes' four dogs, is practically exigent. The inscription above the library at Trajan's Forum in Rome comes to mind: "Dispensary to the Soul," it reads. With books and more books all around, I feel as if I'm absorbing their wisdom by mere proximity—that I've glimpsed the soul of this eminently Southern family. By all means, we are what we read.

Tina and Rob bought their home, designed by famed Louisiana architect A. Hays Town, about eight years ago. "It was in wonderful condition," Rob explains, "but that's how all Mr. Town's homes were built—with a classic frame to withstand the ages." Rob is originally from New Orleans, the big city on the other side of the Mississippi with a culture as rich as its gumbo . . . "but not as rich as it is down here," boasts Tina, a proud native of Abbeville, a tiny, historic town just twenty miles south. "Ever since I was a child, I've dreamt of living in a Hays Town home." And who can blame her? Town had an uncanny ability to incorporate the region's variations of French-colonial homes into comfortable, contemporary, and uniquely Louisiana design. Everything about his style seems authentically

ABOVE: Exposed beams and a recycled pine frame add a sense of rustic charm to this sitting room and adjoining kitchen. The dark feel of the cypress cabinetry, brick floors, and old farmhouse table is lightened with a pair of blue toile chairs.

OPPOSITE: Warm, sophisticated living room vignettes lie beneath the home's strong architectural bones. Recycled pine beams and a rising brick fireplace are signature touches of A. Hays Town and recall the French-colonial style so characteristic of Louisiana's design heritage.

OVERLEAF: The long porch that lines the rear of the house and looks out onto Vermillion Bayou is given the same intimate attention as any other room in the home.

rooted in landscape and culture—handmade brick inside and out, reclaimed wooden beams, deep roof overhangs, central courtyards destined for evergreenery, painted brick, and porch space galore.

Tina and Rob's home on Vermillion Bayou wraps around a courtyard in the front; the back is lined with tall French doors opening onto a verdant and much-frequented porch. Looking around the home, it's no surprise that for more than ten years, Tina was an avid antiques dealer, specializing in English period furniture. "I've been an Anglophile forever—many, many years before Rob and I ever traveled to England," Tina explains. "I think it grew out of my fascination with the Brontës and Jane Austen. I became simply agog with the English disposition and their sophisticated interiors from their writing." But, Tina adds, "A British antique dealer in the heart of Cajun-French country was quite the anomaly." One glance inside Tina's home, however, and it's obvious that a French legacy and British élan can harmonize quite beautifully.

The patina of well-loved books and handpicked period furniture throughout the home wraps around you in a tender, comforting embrace. Rooms are crowded, but elegantly so, without ever being overdressed or underthought. "I've collected for so many years," Tina says, "and even though the kids are grown and—oh dear, don't remind me!—gone, our favorite pieces and our clan of canines keep the atmosphere cozy and alive." There's the boy-girl pair of terra-cotta busts brought from Belgium by her daughter ("Poor Molly," Tina says. "The girl bust arrived at my door decapitated!"), a George IV dining table that holds weekly dinners for family and friends, fleets of Chinese export porcelain—displaying magnolia leaves from the front yard,

Porch Living

A wave to the neighbors passing by, fresh iced tea, and long chats in the late afternoon. Rocking alone on a cool summer evening or curled up on your grandmother's wicker chair with a book. The sun rises and sets, the fan twirls 'round and 'round, the hammock sways, the leaves whisper, and the crickets hum . . . oh, darlin', what on earth is better than a Southern porch?

Whether front, back, side, or screened, the porch connects our indoor and outdoor worlds and provides hospitable space for casual living. And although it's a widespread architectural feature, stretching all the way back to the portico in ancient Greece, porch living *is* a uniquely Southern phenomenon. In the South, and especially before the age of air-conditioning, the warm climate drew Southerners outdoors. It offered shade from the hot sun, refuge from afternoon showers, and cool breezes in the evenings.

The Southern porch is a bridge of sorts between our home and the community, or our home and the outdoors. From the porch, we invite friends to talk (or gossip) until night falls. No need for television. The vistas from the porch, whether a busy street or a quiet marsh, are entertainment enough. But almost above all, porch living depends on those classic porch elements: rockers, porch swings, hammocks, gliders, and wicker . . . lots of wicker. Like much of the interior furniture in Southern homes, outdoor pieces are coveted possessions, often handed down from generation to generation, with pedigrees as rich as our antique silver. Usually movement-oriented and oversized, porch furniture is the foundation for our outdoor rooms, perfectly aligned so that we can see everything going on beyond the porch's edge. Small tables are placed beside the chairs to hold a glass of fresh lemonade or a plate stacked with cucumber sandwiches. Ceiling or table fans circulate the South's stuffy air. Ah, porch living—it's absolutely divine. —*P.S.W.*

LEFT: Layers of creams and golds harmonize with blue toile and floral to create a nurturing, feminine bedroom. The blue-and-white quilt has adorned three generations of Rowe beds, and the mahogany bed was handmade in New Orleans, where Tina and Rob lived before moving to Cajun country. The botanicals were collected by Tina's daughter while living in France.

them as often as possible—they only get prettier with use." And, basically, that's how everything is in her home—fine objects approached with an everyday casualness. "I believe that your beautiful pieces— inherited or collected—should fit into your everyday life. It's like your favorite piece of jewelry," Tina explains. "It may be special and cost a fortune, but, darling, that's all the more reason to wear it

arranged atop the mantel, or underneath a demilune table—and black-and-white family portraits galore. Indeed, the copper bucket filled to the brim with well-loved dog toys is awarded the same pride of place as the Dutch oils hanging above. "It's wonderful to be surrounded by our children and great memories at every turn," Rob says as he follows the aroma of Tina's crawfish étouffée from the kitchen. I try to pick up a few Cajun cuisine secrets from an adjoining sitting room casually dressed in blue toile, soft floral, and antique leather. Tina adds more (and more and more) spice . . . of course.

All around the home, delicious sweets abound: fresh banana-nut bread to my left, homemade pralines to my right, canning jars with gingham lids in the pantry—"We're making blackberry preserves tomorrow," Tina tells me as she pours us a glass of water in her engraved mint julep cups. "I started collecting these right out of college, and I try to use

ABOVE LEFT: A tall stack of biographies lies within arm's reach of this long-seated nineteenth-century British chair in Tina and Rob's bedroom. A Coromandel screen adds depth to the composition, while a Louis XVI mirror atop an oak mule chest with walnut inlay adds height to a low ceiling.

ABOVE: The English secretary is filled with books and personal memorabilia, such as Tina's father's childhood glasses resting on an open book.

The glow of one room propels you with curiosity into the next.

While centuries of artists, tourists, and bon vivants have flocked to New Orleans to peek into her Creole soul, relatively few have ventured down the bayou to Acadiana—a petite pocket of French heritage descending from about a hundred French families deported from the Bay of Fundy (today, Nova Scotia) by the British in the late seventeenth century. Today, the culture is famed for its high-spirited family gatherings, distinctly flavored cuisine, and much-anticipated festivals, celebrating anything from crawfish to Zydeco music. The joie de vivre in and around Lafayette, Louisiana, is, without a doubt, contagious. One step inside the Saitta home, and you would have to agree.

Sinking into a down-filled sofa in the living room, wide-eyed and enthralled, I'm enchanted by the decorative embellishments and otherworldliness of the place. The urge to touch is unbearable. The craving to stay just a bit longer is palpable. The warmth exuding from the colorfully cocooned atmosphere is endearing. This enclave of casual elegance has enough personality to stimulate a smile from everyone on *this* side of the Mississippi.

With an impressionist's color palette and a touch of je ne sais quoi, Anita and Vince Saitta have fashioned a home that is as intimate as it is beautiful. And although each room has an exquisite European accent, the home speaks unabashedly to its Southern heritage. "Our home is built around our favorite pieces and the stories they tell . . . memories that tie this piece with that, memories that make this painting so special, or that chair my

ABOVE: The simple, dark brick exterior is a surprising shell for the Saittas' home, which is resplendent with vivid color, lusty Italian music, and echoes of laughter.

OPPOSITE: A romantic harmony of reds, raspberries, deep pinks, and delicate tableware passed down through the generations exudes an elegant air. The round table is set to serve apéritifs. The portrait of Anita and Vince's three children is by William Carl Groh III.

favorite," Anita says. "Without a story weaving it all together, it's just *brocante* or, even worse, vacuous design." In the living room, all eyes are drawn to a striking portrait of Joyce Blanchet Guilliot, Anita's mother. "They called her Joyce-Tee," she explains. "Her brother was T-Paul and her sister, Mary Boo. No name is complete in Cajun-French culture without an extra syllable for endearment."

Anita, an interior decorator who owns Saitta Interiours, has mastered the art of elevating the everyday to the *raffiné*. Place cards from wonderful dinners tucked into the frame of a belle epoque *trumeau* are given the same pride of place as the inherited gems. Her oldest daughter's wedding invitation, written in French; a first communion prayer book held by four generations of Blanchet/Guilliot/Saitta women; small statuettes of St. Francis and the Madonna; and her

ABOVE: Each intricately designed curtain is adorned with Anita's signature touch: antique buttons from a jar in her mother-in-laws' attic and a small ladybug for good luck.

LEFT: A Provençal color palette infuses the breakfast room with creative energy and French flair. A collection of white faience plates brightens the walls. The drapery is composed of seven different vintage fabrics and tied back with crushed canning jar lids.

grandmother's clock are aligned with a tilt of nostalgia along the living room mantel. Somehow, this visual memoir inspires an odd clairvoyance—the family heritage, the laughter arising from wonderful evenings, the rich memories of raising three children within these walls are sensed whether or not you know exactly what the story entails. It's warm, it's piquant, it's extremely personal yet all inviting, and the glow of one room propels you with curiosity into the next.

If there's a single unifying theme, it's a passion for color. There's no cream-colored wall or neutral-toned slipcover in sight. "No one is quiet in my family—we're all vivacious," Anita says. But should you meet any of them, you'd be charmed by their natural gentility and sparkling *politesse*. "To fill my house with neutrals wouldn't fit who we are. We're a colorful group." Yet Anita did not opt for merely the brightly colored wall or the patterned fabric. She opted for them all . . . and then more. The living room features raspberry walls and over-stuffed Italianate sofas and chairs upholstered in rose-colored toile and vibrant floral, stacked high with a panoply of pillows covered in vintage fabrics. For the sitting area just off the kitchen, it's a Provençal blend of blues and yellows. The curtains alone are composed of seven different fabrics; the

ABOVE RIGHT: In a home atelier, functional organization is synonymous with welcoming design. Pillows and lampshades awaiting purchase hang whimsically from the ceiling and the door.

RIGHT: A mélange of memorabilia—from place cards to wedding invitations—enlivens the mantel and *trumeau* with personal *douende*. The mantel was custom painted by artist William Carl Groh III.

Fortuny fringe found in Florence. Worn, often peeling surfaces of outdoor ornaments are elevated to an unexpected finery when placed beside the elegant curves of France and Italy. "I like mixing the elegant with the alfresco," she explains, "blending 'unmatched' textures together in a way that defies the written rules, but turns out absolutely perfect to the eye."

Although the children are grown and the upstairs bedrooms aren't nearly as lively, Anita and Vince still welcome convivial traffic into their home on an almost routine basis. From mid-morning until late at night, friends and family and members of Saitta Interiours' decorating team parade in and out of the front, back, and side doors. They curl up in club chairs, then, perhaps, stroll to the back porch for a glass of iced tea . . . then it's to the kitchen stools for an afternoon nibble or an early apéritif. "This house is our home," Anita explains, "but we want everyone who walks through the door to feel comfortable here, too." And, as we laugh and smile and don't ever want to leave, indeed we do. —*P.S.W.*

sofa boasts five. A semiovular arrangement of faience plates covers an entire wall, brightening the room even more. "My mother gave me one plate for each birthday as I was growing up," Anita explains, "and I began the same tradition for my two daughters."

While it's easy to notice Anita's affinity for all that is French, upon closer inspection, her Italian panache shines through as well. "I'm French, but Vince is Italian. Our home is like our family—a marriage of both cultures." There's the simple pairing of beautiful pieces, such as the Italianate buffet beside a French *vaisselier* in the dining room. But the charm of this European union stems from more personal compositions, like the French lovebirds beneath the Florentine coffee table that Anita gave Vince as an anniversary gift, or a bedspread made from vintage toile found in Provence, edged with

ABOVE: Old cypress fencing encloses a small, welcoming side garden.

OPPOSITE: A collection of silver domes animates the floor beneath this Louis XV polychrome *écritoire*, an intriguing replacement for the traditional coffee table. No space goes ignored.

RIGHT: Exquisite window treatments and "Virgin Mary blue" walls set the stage for a dramatic master bedroom. From the bedspread with sectional quilting to the Jackie O–inspired lampshade, every square inch is designed with meticulous care.

BELOW: A riot of color creates an unexpected pocket of serenity. A Swedish down-filled loveseat is accented with an eclectic arrangement of pillows made from vintage fabrics. Anita's mother's bronze sconces frame a belle epoque *trumeau* layered with paint and glaze to resemble ivory parquetry.

Index

Italic page numbers indicate photography